RESOURCES

OF THE

STATE OF ARKANSAS,

WITH

DESCRIPTION OF COUNTIES,

RAIL ROADS, MINES,

AND THE

CITY OF LITTLE ROCK,

THE COMMERCIAL, MANUFACTURING, POLITICAL AND
RAIL ROAD CENTER OF THE STATE.

BY JAMES P. HENRY.

LITTLE ROCK, ARK.
PRICE & McCLURE, PRINTERS.
1872.

DEDICATION.

TO THE STATE OF ARKANSAS AND CITY OF LITTLE ROCK.

Of Arkansas little has been written, and little is known outside its borders. The State of Arkansas—the least known but most inviting to immigrants, because presenting a climate the most lovely in the Union, a soil the most reproductive in all the fruits of the earth; mineral resources second to none in richness and extent; timber, the most useful in all the mechanical arts, and farms, of one hundred and sixty arces, to be had simply for the asking—a State containing all the elements of an empire within itself, the City of Little Rock, "the future great city of the southwest," located on the world's highway from the Atlantic to the Pacific, on the national highway from the north to the south; in the center of a State that can furnish happy homes for 5,000,000 of people; on the chief river of Arkansas, surrounded by a country the most lovely of Uncle Sam's domain; located on a hill, receiving the full benefit of the health-inspiring breezes; the city of railroads, and the city that is destined to outstrip all her rivals, this work, devoted to the advancement and development of the material resources of Arkansas, is dedicated by the

AUTHOR.

TABLE OF CONTENTS.

EXPLANATORY.

Post masters and citizens generally, throughout Arkansas, are daily receiving numerous letters of inquiry about Arkansas; its soil, minerals, manufactories and climate, its healthfulness, progress and resources generally. These are interspersed with questions about rail roads, rail way, government, homestead and pre-emption lands, for farming, fruit growing and stock raising, and for all kinds of pursuits, requiring little or more considerable capital; and the chances for engaging in industrial avocations in a peaceable, moral and law abiding way, among peaceable and law revering people. This pamphlet is issued for the purpose of aiding to answer such inquiries, and to encourage the development of the resources of Arkansas, the prosperity and material advancement of the State, and that its manifold resources, inducements and advantages to immigrants, may be made known to the outside world, who know comparatively little about this State. And will furnish under separate and distinct heads, information to the world, on the climate, soil, minerals, products, etc., of Arkansas, which cannot fail to be of immense advantage to persons looking for new homes with a view of bettering their condition in life. And also, will be the means of adding greatly to the wealth and population of Arkansas; a State that henceforth will increase faster in population and wealth than any of the States in the Mississippi valley, by reason of her favorable situation between the warm latitude of the south and the icy plains of the north a State, the most inviting to immigrants, because offering the greatest inducements.

J. P. H.

HISTORICAL FACTS OF ARKANSAS.

The Commissioner of the United States Land Office, says:

"West of the Mississippi river, in the State of Arkansas, lies an extremely fertile, well watered country, occasionally mountainous, and at other times level; being one of the most productive regions on the continent for the culture of cotton, corn and tobacco. The products of Arkansas are classed with those of agriculture, manufactures, the forest and the mines; of the first, the variety is great, embracing the hardy growth of the northern, in the western, and the tropical plants and fruits of the south, in the eastern and southern sections. The principal of these are wheat, rye, oats, sweet and Irish potatoes, maize, peas, beans, butter, cheese, wool, slaughtered animals, honey, bees-wax, tobacco, cotton, hay and garden products of great number and value."

Governor Conway, in his annual message to the Legislature of 1858, says:

"If we had labor enough to cultivate all the cotton lands in the State, Arkansas alone, could supply, annually, the market of the world, with as much cotton as has ever been raised any year, in all of the cotton growing States of the Union." This is equally true to-day.

RESOURCES OF ARKANSAS.

ARKANSAS HISTORY.

Arkansas was settled by the French, in the year 1670, and was purchased from the French in the Louisiana acquisition of 1803; was created a territory, March 2, 1819, and admitted as a State in the Union, June 15, 1836. Arkansas had a population in 1820, of fourteen thousand; in 1830, of thirty thousand; in 1840, of ninety-seven thousand; in 1850, of two hundred and nine thousand; in 1869, of four hundred and thirty-five thousand; in 1870, of four hundred and eighty-five thousand; or about nine and a half to the square mile; and is capable of sustaining a population of more than one hundred to the square mile.

Every person conversant with the geography of the United States, dont doubt the capacity of Arkansas, to sustain as large a population as Massachusetts, to the square mile. Massachusetts, with an area of 7,800 square miles, equal to 4,992,000 acres, sustains a population of 1,457,354, about 158 to the square mile. Arkansas, with an area of 52,198 square miles, equal to 33,406,720 acres, contained in 1870, only 485,000 inhabitants; and give Arkansas 158 to the square mile, and she will furnish happy homes for 8,247,284 people. Arkansas is the least known and most abused State in the Union. The ignorance of this State is not surprising, when one takes into consideration, that in 1860 there were just 38½ miles of railroad, and in 1870, January 1, just 128 miles of completed railroads. And the vast interior country, between the navigable rivers was almost unknown to the outside world, and, in times past, furnished a safe retreat for those who had reason to fear the law; but this state of things has passed away. Ruffianism has seen its day here. The inhabitants comprise people from all the States, and are as moral and law-abiding as anywhere. Society is good, and the people are all concerned about their material interest.

Here is a vast and rich region which has been of little importance to the rest of the world. But, since the war closed in 1865, a new era has dawned upon this beautiful country; now comes railroads! What a change is soon to take place; the bottoms, valleys and hills, now so sparsely settled, will be populated with a thriving and industrious people, and her rich metal and mineral resources will be developed, adding greatly to the prosperity of the whole country. Under the old regime of slavery, Arkansas was left far behind in the march of empire. The northwestern States, possessing far less natural resources and advantages, was fast filling up by immigrants from the eastern States and the old world; and it is only since 1867 that this state of things is being changed by the multitude of emigrants, who are seeking homes in our mild and pleasant climate, and upon our fruitful soil. Arkansas, during the war, was not only drained of her material wealth, but of multitudes of people; but the return of peace and the increased and ever increasing tide of immigration, will bring the State up to at least one million inhabitants by the year 1880. Of the present inhabitants of Arkansas, about one hundred and twenty-two thousand are colored. Considering the condition these people have been in, for generations past, they have conducted themselves with great propriety since their formal emancipation, in 1865. A large majority of them are not only making an honest support for themselves and families, but, by their industry and frugality, accumulating a decent competence. The State was thrown back in her industrial career by the war; but it is gratifying to notice that the people have met the crisis with admirable fortitude; and there is the best reason for believing that a change, the beginning of which is already perceptible, will be wrought in the habits of the people, and prove eminently salutary and beneficial. Another effect will be the disintegration of the overgrown and unwieldy plantations, and their subdivision into small farms. The time will come when this grand State will be dotted over with thousands of happy abodes, and her fair surface literally transformed into a garden. Such is the picture that will assuredly be presented when the great natural resources and advantages of the country are developed to their full extent.

Arkansas is recuperating at a wonderful rate; her geographical position, her rich and productive soil, her inexhaustible underground wealth, and her mild and salubrious climate, justly entitle her to be fitly called the Switzerland of the southwest.

RESOURCES OF ARKANSAS.

Arkansas is centrally situated in the United States, from east to west, and a little south of the center from north to south. Her wonderful rich resources, when once developed, will make her the Empire State of the southwest. Her climatic situation is propitious, the State lying between the temperate parallels of 33 and 36 deg. north latitude, and between the meridians of 89 deg. 40 min. and 94 deg. 42 min. west longitude. The dimensions of the State embrace an area of 52,198 square miles, equal to 33,406,720 acres of land, about the size of England, and surpassing the productive capacity of that wonderful country, and possessing as much arable and fruitful soil as any of her sister States of the Mississippi valley.

About one third of her 33,406,720 acres of land is still owned by the United States, and can be taken up under the homestead law. No State is better supplied with water powers and navigable rivers. Arkansas is bounded on the east by the Mississippi river, bisected by the Arkansas. The White, Black, St. Francis and Ouachita all flow through this State into the Mississippi, and are navigable for steamboats three-fourths of the year. Nature has given to Arkansas vast resources in agricultural and mineral wealth; also, facilities for managing the internal commerce of the State and the southwest.

The western and northern portions are somewhat broken, the country sometimes appearing as broad table-lands, and then again broken into rough and rugged hills. Most of the latter are rich in metals and minerals. The greater portion of this broken, hilly region is susceptible of cultivation, and for stock raising, or the growing of the cereals, fruits, and especially the grape, no better land can be found anywhere.

The first settlers of Arkansas generally sought the rich alluvial soils of the eastern and southern portions, for the cultivation of cotton. This vast fruitful and mineral region of the northern and western portions were neglected. However, that time has passed, and thousands of immigrants, both farmers and miners, are making pleasant and profitable homes in this part of the State. Here is the fruit grower's paradise; fruits of all kinds grow to perfection. The natural conditions demanded by the fruits are soil and climate; given these, the others will follow, from the application of the skillful grower. In all this portion of the State these two elementary conditions, soil and climate, exist together. That the growing of fruits in Arkansas is destined to be an immense business, is a fact beyond a doubt. The fruits of north Arkansas, for size and flavor, are not excelled by any State in the Union.

The soil along the creek and river bottoms is as rich as any in the world; and her upland soil is equally as rich as the soil of Missouri, Iowa or Wisconsin.

Arkansas has been, and is now, a cotton growing State; cotton is her staple product. Her rich alluvial soils of the creek and river bottoms produce from one to one and a half bales to the acre, which rarely brings less than seventy dollars per bale. More corn has been grown this year than ever before; and instead of corn being an article of import, as heretofore, this necessary article will be grown where it is needed, a home product. Wheat, oats, barley, rye, Irish and sweet potatoes, the grasses, timothy, clover, red top, all grow well and produce good crops.

THE IMMIGRANT

From the north to Arkansas, may see growing on the same farm, cotton, corn, wheat, oats, clover, timothy, vegetables, both northern and southern varieties, fruits, such as apples, peaches, pears, plums, cherries, apricots, nectarines, grapes, strawberries, etc.

The capacity of this State for producing cotton, and the food for both man and animals, is something enormous. Whenever the resources of the State are fully developed, Arkansas will furnish happy homes for a population of five millions of people, one half producing food not only for themselves but to feed the other half, who will be engaged as miners, mechanics, etc., and the State every year exporting more than she imports.

THE PEOPLE OF ARKANSAS,

Hitherto, have been strictly an agricultural people. No mining or manufacturing has been carried on in any portion of the State to any extent worth mentioning; but now, the railroads built and under construction, with the favorable laws passed by the last Legislature, encouraging mining and manufacturing, are working wonderful changes in the vocations of the people. Mining villages are being established, and manufacturing companies organized in various portions of the State.

OF ARKANSAS

Little has been written, and little is known outside its borders, for the reason it has never been the interest of any to publish to the world its excellencies. Formerly, when slavery existed, the land owners were its tillers, and would not dispose of any of their fine lands, but would add to and enlarge their plantations, studiously concealing and avoiding publicity as to the

great richness of soil and advantages of climate from the outside world, which no one blames them for. But a great change has taken place since slavery has been abolished; the land owners, generally, find they have too much land, and gladly welcome the immigrant, from every clime, "as fellow-workers in the fertile fields" of Arkansas. Immigrants nowhere in the United States will be more honored, respected and encouraged than by the citizens and land owners of Arkansas; and nowhere else are the inducements so varied and so great to those who desire to better their condition in life, alike to all, farmers, mechanics, laborers; and to the capitalist, Arkansas offers peculiar advantages. Taking the State with all its advantages, its fruitful soil, its mild and healthy climate, its vast mineral wealth, its facilities for transportation, both by river and rail, and there is no State in the Union that offers superior inducements for the investment of capital, the founding of new enterprises and the securing of permanent homes.

THE CLIMATE.

"The climate of Arkansas is peculiar. Being situated almost half way between the great southern gulf, and the semi-artic regions of the north," therefore, she is blessed with a climate not only good, but delightful—between the extremes of heat and cold—presenting a climate, the most lovely in the world. The winters are short and mild, and the summers pleasant; the winter months resemble the fall months of the north. To those who have spent a score of years in the north, contending with snow and ice from November until April, will be perfectly delighted with our winters, almost a continual Indian summer. Our summers are longer than at the north, but not so hot. We are free from headache and sun strokes brought on by heat. Laborers work in the sun all day, without feeling any exhaustation from its effects. No country in the world furnishes a larger number of days in the year, in which out door work can be performed. "In the hottest days of summer, there is usually a cooling breeze from the west. The nights, always cool, make the hottest days quite endurable to the tired laborer, falling into the arms of balmy sleep—nature's sweet restorer."

Our winters are so mild that stock live upon grass and cane of the bottoms all winter, without being taken up, and without food or expense to the owners. In fact, our beef is slaughtered from the cane pastures, on the numerous creek and river bottoms. We have the finest autumns in the world. The Indian summer generally lasts until the middle of January; then we have a few inches of snow, usually lying on the ground only a few days, the ground seldom freezing deeper than two or three inches. A cold wind now and then, but never do we have those cold, penetrating winds of the north-west, that seem to freeze up the marrow in your bones. We are also free from drouths in summer, and those extremes of wet and dry seasons, peculiar to the latitudes north of us. Arkansas challenges the world, not only in the beauty of her climate, but in the various agricultural productions, the natural richness of soil, and in variety and wealth of mineral deposits.

We can strongly recommend this State to the immigrant. There is room in this beautiful country for thousands, where land is cheap, labor is cheap, stock is cheap, life and property secure, society good, and the State must, ere long, take rank in point of wealth and population with the richest in the Mississippi valley. Arkansas will soon be enrolled as a prosperous member in the Union. Yes, Arkansas is making rapid strides in the way of general improvements. Where is there a better opportunity for investment, either by the capitalist, or the man who wishes to have a home of his own, "where he can sit under his own vine and fig tree, and eat the wholesome and honest bread of independence?" The small or large farmers, living on the worn out lands of the south or east, or the frugal farmers of the north-west, in search of a mild and pleasant climate, rich and productive soil, soft and pure water, will please make a note of this! Some may still ask, is

ARKANSAS HEALTHY?

To all, I assure, this State is decidedly healthy for a State having no more of her domain cleared and under cultivation. As the country becomes more thickly settled, and brought under cultivation, the health of the country will correspondingly improve. In the fall of the year, a mild type of chills and fever affects some of the inhabitants, particularly those who are careless, or happen to live in malarious localities: while billious diseases, incident to all new countries, is here almost unknown. The soft, mellow, pure air is singularly beneficial to persons pre-disposed to consumption or bronchial affections. Many enjoy health here who have been given up to die in the north. As regards health, this climate is unsurpassed, and among the chief excellencies it offers the strongest recommendation for settlement, pulmonary diseases very rarely originate here. Those who will live upon low bottoms, out of the way of the health giving breezes, may expect to have a touch of fever and ague occasionally. There is a health giving power in the sun and atmosphere here, that must be experienced to be appreciated.

The mercury in the thermometer, during the winter months, sometimes comes down to 16 or 10 degrees above, but very rarely gets to zero; a point it has not reached in the last five years. And, during the hot months, it sometimes goes up to 90, but rarely ever gets up to 100 degrees. The meteorology report of the State for 1870, taken at the center of the State, by daily observations, generally at 7 A. M., 2 and 9 P. M., show the maximum, minimum and average temperature for every month in the year to be as follows:

Months.	Maximum.	Date.	Minimum.	Av. Tem.
January	72 deg.	9 to 19	26 deg.	45 d.
February	69 deg.	15 to 20	14 deg.	46 d. 4 m.
March	73 deg.	9 to 24	26 deg.	49 d. 1 m.
April	84 deg.	16 to 22	33 deg.	61 d. 3m.
May	93 deg.	7 to 23	52 deg.	71d. 8m.
June	94 deg.	8 to 22	60 deg.	76 d. 5m.
July	94 deg.	8 to 16	68 deg.	81 d. 8m.
August	90 deg.	13 to 30	69 deg.	81 d. 4m.
September	96 deg.	6 to 28	59 deg.	76 d. 6m.
October	87 deg.	20 to 30	42 deg.	63 d. 7m.
November	86 deg.	4 to 26	31 deg.	54 d. 8m.
December	73 deg.	7 to 24	4 deg.	38 d. 5m.

Now we will compare the temperature of the State of Iowa, taken at Dubuque, and any one can see which has the most even temperature, and the most inviting climate for permanent settlement, and where out door labor can be performed with less suffering from extremes of either heat or cold; and where, as a matter of course, the health of the people is correspondingly affected:

Months.	Maximum.	Date.	Minimum.	Av. Tem.
January..................	43 deg.	16 to 17.	6d. below.	21 d. 2m.
February.................	51 deg.	20 to 26.	7 do.	25 d. 8m.
March....................	52 deg.	16 to 28.	4 do.	30 d. 8m.
April....................	82 deg.	13 to 24.	28 degrees.	52 d. 9m.
May......................	87 deg.	3 to 22.	48 deg.	67 d.
June.....................	102 deg.	7 to 29.	56 deg.	74 d. 5m.
July.....................	100 deg.	25 to 30.	58 deg.	77 d. 9m.
August...................	95 deg.	5 to 20.	51 deg.	70 d. 8m.
September................	88 deg.	7 to 19.	51 deg.	65 d. 9m.
October..................	72 deg.	1 to 31.	26 deg.	50 d. 7m.
November.................	60 deg.	6 to 22.	22 deg.	39 d. 7m.
December.................	51 deg,	1 to 23,	12d. below.	24 d.

The above tables show that the mercury goes up a great deal higher in summer and very much lower, say 16 to 24 degrees, in winter, in the State of Iowa than it does in Arkansas. Then, again, we have four seasons in Arkansas—spring, summer, fall and winter. Spring weather commences in February and lasts until June; summer comes from June until September, then fall, from September to December, and lastly a short winter, from December 1st to February, two months, and that, too, like October in Iowa, whilst in the northwest they really have but two seasons, summer and winter. When winter breaks, there are about ten days or two weeks of rainy, cloudy and awful muddy weather, then summer comes in, as far as heat is concerned, and lasts until September, when winter again sets in long and fierce until April. The spring and fall seasons are so short that there really can't be more than a month that can be called spring or fall months. And again, it takes a man's hard summer's work to make grain to feed himself, and especially his stock, during the long winter, and then barely sufficient to keep the hides on the frame. The northwestern States can never compete with Arkansas, because the winters eat up the fruits of the summers' labor.

AGRICULTURAL RESOURCES.

There is probably no State in the American Union that enjoys greater natural advantages for the production of a great variety of the fruits of the earth than Arkansas. Situated in the most favored parallels of the temperate zone, with a wide diversity of soils, and blessed with a climate for the most part eminently salubrious, it is capable of meeting the requirements of every variety of rural taste and of sustaining a dense population. The agricultural products of Arkansas are varied and great, and well adapted to a diversified agriculture and the varied employments of man. There are millions of acres of land still unimproved, that only await the hand of the laborer to make them productive of immense wealth to the owners and the country. It must be remembered this State is so situated that there is, with few exceptions, no product of the soil pertaining to the temperate or tropical zones, and which is of real use to man as food, which cannot be grown in this State. The evidences of the accumulation of wealth and the increase of production in other States of the Union, show unmistakably that those States adapted to mixed agriculture and employ the time and capital of the farmer twelve months in the year, are the most profitable ones. A farmer can here raise a crop with about one-half the labor and expense that is required in the north or east. For those desiring a pleasant, profitable and healthful employment in the most salubrious of all climates, where he can labor in the open air every day in the year, and where he can maintain himself so easily with limited means until he can improve his farm; when that is done, the reward for his labor will be great, and himself independent. More money can be made farming in Arkansas than in the northwest; *First.* Because of the greater variety of crops produced; *Second.* We are several hundred miles nearer the great consuming regions of the south and the shipping ports for the West Indies and Europe; *Third.* Because in a short time a home market, the best of all markets, will be built up in our midst, by reason of our great mineral wealth, capable of sustaining an untold number of miners and manufacturers.

The report of the agricultural products of Arkansas, compared with other States of the Mississippi valley, based upon the census returns of 1870, are highly favorable for Arkansas. According to the annual report of the Department of Agriculture:

ARKANSAS.

	Amt. of crop.	Av. yield per acre.	Val. per bu., ton, lb.
Indian corn	25,000,000 bush.	$31\frac{1}{3}$	$ 80
Wheat	1,500,000 "	$10\frac{1}{8}$	1 30
Rye	41,600 "	$18\frac{1}{2}$	1 00
Oats	671,000 "	$23\frac{1}{6}$	62
Potatoes	450,000 "	109	1 07
Tobacco	2,225,000 lbs.	666	$15\frac{1}{3}$
Hay	10,200 tons	$1\frac{1}{2}$	15 00

STOCK.

	Number.	Average price.
Horses	138,100	$73 98
Mules	67,900	93 51
Oxen and other cattle	221,900	11 82
Milch cows	132,600	22 14
Sheep	135,000	2 32
Hogs	863,600	3 28

MISSOURI.

	Amt. of crop.	Av. yield per acre.	Val. per bu., ton, lb.
Indian corn	94,960,000 bush.	$31\frac{1}{4}$	$ 44
Wheat	6,750,000 "	13	91
Rye	299,000 "	$15\frac{1}{6}$	68
Oats	5,525,000 "	25	37
Barley	285,000 "	$26\frac{1}{4}$	84
Buckwheat	84,000 "	$23\frac{1}{6}$	67
Potatoes	2,200,000 "	103	56
Tobacco	19,610,000 lbs.	750	$09\frac{1}{8}$
Hay	532,000 tons.	1 1-5	12 82

STOCK.

	Number.	Average price.
Horses	483,000	$63 61
Mules	83,400	83 43
Oxen and other cattle	731,100	24 46
Milch cows	371,200	31 92
Sheep	1,578,200	1 61
Hogs	2,200,000	4 34

KANSAS.

	Amt. of crop.	Av. yield per acre.	Val. per bu., ton, lb.
Indian corn	16,685,000 bush.	28	$ 58
Wheat	2,343,000 "	15	86
Rye	77,500 "	$20\frac{1}{8}$	69
Oats	3,688,000 "	31 1-5	40
Barley	92,500 "	24	75
Buckwheat	31,000 "	$20\frac{1}{6}$	77
Potatoes	3,139,000 "	106	56
Hay	529,000 tons	1 1-5	7 18

STOCK.

	Number.	Average price
Horses	156,000	$72 15
Mules	14,900	92 14
Oxen and other cattle	345,600	28 84
Milch cows	162,000	38 46
Sheep	115,000	2 58
Hogs	304,800	8 88

TEXAS.

	Am't of Crop. Bsh'l.	Av'ge Yield per Acre.	Value per bs'l, ton, lb.
Indian corn	23,690,000	26 1-5	$1 06
Wheat	1,225,000	11 1-7	1 78
Rye	95,000	19	1 11
Barley	54,000	30	1 33
Oats	1,500,000	21 1-6	1 00
Potatoes	400,000	128	1 33
Hay—tons	25,000	1 6-10	15 36

STOCK.

	Number.	Av. Price.
Horses	615,700	$32 29
Mules	82,900	52 30
Oxen and other cattle	3,220,000	7 37
Milch cows,	596,500	12 83
Sheep,	1,137 300	1 40
Hogs,	1,200,000	2 76

Buckwheat and barley are not enumerated in Arkansas, for the reason that heretofore they have not been considered necessary farm crops, but large and profitable crops of both, are now, and can be grown. There is not a county in the State in which the cereals, fruits and vegetables, cannot be grown in great abundance. Indeed there is scarcely a limit to the food-producing capabilities of the soil of the State. If the immigrant desires cotton land, he can have it in the rich alluvial bottoms; if he wants grain land, he can have it in the rich soil of the uplands; or does he wish fruit land, if so, he can have a choice of thousands of acres of the finest fruit lands in the Union, now covered with wild grape vines, some of which will make six rails to the cut. Now, what shall be said of Arkansas that produces cotton, corn, wheat, oats, rye, barley, hay, Irish and sweet potatoes, and all the vegetables.

COTTON.

The broad river bottoms, composed of a rich sandy loam, easily cultivated and very fertile, furnish the finest cotton growing lands in the south, and are becoming immensely valuable, producing from one to one and a half bales to the acre, and after some of them have been in cultivation from twenty to fifty years, show little or no sign of deterioration, as compared with the virgin soil. The farmer starts his plows generally the first week after new years, and cotton is planted from the first of March until the middle of April. One hand with a one horse plow can cultivate thirteen acres of cotton, or ten acres of cotton and five acres of corn. The cultivating is about the same as for corn, and is laid by about the first of

June, and cotton picking commences about the first of October, and continues until the crop is saved. A good crop to sell, as the farmer can haul to market at one load, the product of three or four acres. All the children from five years old can be efficiently employed in the cultivating and picking; cotton worth now from 18 to 20 cents per pound, averaging about ninety dollars per bale.

CORN.

The bottom lands produce from 40 to 75 bushels, and the uplands from 30 to 60 bushels to the acre. The land can be broken any time from first of January, and corn can be planted from February until June, but the usual time for planting is the month of March; 20 acres to the hand is the usual crop. By the use of sulky cultivators 40 acres can be tended; it is ripe September the first, and generally all cribbed before cotton picking commences. The average yield of the whole State in 1869 was 31 1-8 bushels, and average price 80 cents; the price runs from 50 cents to one dollar per bushel, with not enough raised for home consumption generally.

WHEAT.

The upland soil of most portions of the State produces a superior article of wheat; the kernel is remarkably heavy and flinty, and weighs from 60 to 65 pounds to the measured bushel. Statistics show that the best flour is made from wheat grown south of 38 deg. north latitude. Arkansas flour is conceded by every person who has used it, to be superior to the best imported article from Saint Louis. The yield of wheat to the acre in some counties is 30 bushels, and in others 20 bushels, and even lower per acre, depending in a great measure upon the soil, mode of preparing the land and the season; worth from $1 25 to $1 50 per bushel.

RYE.

Northern Arkansas produces fine crops of rye, and the growing of this grain is fast increasing in area of acres; it yields from 10 to 30 bushels to the acre, worth about $1 00 per bushel.

BARLEY AND BUCKWHEAT

Is grown to some extent, and the soil is well adapted to their cultivation, especially northern Arkansas.

OATS

Grow well and produces large crops, the yield varying from 20 to 40 bushels to the acre; the crop is planted in January and February, worth from 50 to 75 cents per bushel.

HAY

From timothy, red top and clover, have as yet not received much attention, because of the great abundance of wild hay; but there are thousands of acres of land in Arkansas well adapted for the raising of timothy, red top or clover, and wherever they have been tried, the result is very gratifying and the yield from one to three tons to the acre, worth from fifteen to twenty dollars per ton.

At present hay to an unlimited amount can be had on the prairies and bottoms free; each one cuts when or where he pleases, though the only persons needing hay are livery stable keepers and persons living in towns. Farmers absolutely preparing no food for stock during the winter months, and as long as the range is unfenced and uncleared, there is really but little use for devoting time and money to lay up a winter supply.

SORGUM

Is grown in great abundance and produces heavy crops of juicy cane. Sorgum molasses retails from the stores at one dollar per gallon.

PEAS AND BEANS

Grow well and are produced in immense quantities, affording

to the farmer a remunerative field crop, selling at four dollars per bushel.

TOBACCO.

The red upland soils are peculiarly advantageous for the cultivation of tobacco, producing from 1000 to 1500 pounds to the acre. These lands have more than an average of oxide of iron; the same kind of soil as the celebrated Cuba tobacco lands, that produce the fine quality of Havana tobacco. The cultivation of the weed will become a profitable crop in Arkansas, as soil and climate are both favorable.

IRISH POTATOES.

This vegetable grows here as large and fine as in Missouri or Iowa. Northern Arkansas seems well suited to their growth, and in size and flavor are equal to the celebrated Michigan potatoes; they yield, here, from 100 to 200 bushels to the acre, and a very profitable crop to raise, being worth from $1 00 to $2 50 per bushel.

SWEET POTATOES.

Sweet Potatoes are in their native element, being grown in large quantities, of a large size, and of a peculiar good quality, averaging about 150 bushels to the acre, and worth from 50 cents to $1 50 per bushel.

VEGETABLES.

Vegetables, of all kinds, both northern and southern varieties, grow to perfection. Everything in the garden truck line are produced in abundance, and of a good quality; gardens are made both in spring and fall. We have cabbages, turnips, onions, new potatoes, peas, beans, etc., ripe and suitable for the table, from the middle of May on through the season. We produce as large cabbage heads as are grown in the Mississippi valley. I have seen 140 bushels of onions produced from an acre, large, smooth and high flavored as Iowa can do with boasted onion soil near Dubuque. The winters are so mild that we can have lettuce, spinach, green onions, turnip greens, etc., all winter.

PRICES OF FARM PRODUCTS.

The prices of all farm products are high, and as the demand is increasing, fully equal to the increase of supply, there is but little prospect for a reduction in prices. One great advantage this State has over the north-west is, that the farmer has twice as long time to prepare his land and plant his crop. In the north-west, the frost is not out of the ground, and the farmer cannot plow until about the first of April; then he has his wheat and oats to sow, and his corn land to break, and corn must be planted by the middle of May; he has either to plant a small crop, as his time is limited, or keep a large number of teams, plows, etc.. and hire extra hands. Whilst here, he can plow in January, February and March, and sow and plant until May; in fact, there is seldom a day in the winter, the ground cannot be ploughed, if dry enough. Another advantage, the early ripening of vegetables and fruits, enable the growers to command the high prices of the first of the season in all the north-western States, on account of the facility and cheapness with which these products can be marketed, when rail roads now under construction are completed. In about two years time, we will be in direct communication with St. Louis and Kansas City, and thence to all the north-west. Where shall the immigrant seek for better soil, better climate, or more natural advantages? where can he find a better country, all things considered, where moderate labor will give him all the necessaries of life? The rich quality of the soil, the mild and healthy climate, will render this State very desirable for a home.

FRUIT CULTURE.

This State is as fine a fruit country as the sun shines upon. There is something in the soil peculiarly favorable to the production of fruits, giving them a flavor superior to any fruit in the Union. All fruit yields abundant crops, the trees bend under their excessive loads, notwithstanding the fruit crop has not failed in Arkansas for thirty years. The cause of this is attributed to the ridges and valleys of the country, thereby securing a perfect water and air drainage, and complete immunity from late frosts in the spring. Our apples beat the world in size and flavor. We have peaches and pears from the first of June until the first of November; and delicious apricots in June. Our winter apples are hauled to Texas, and sold at a fair profit.

We are located on the fruit belt of the United States. Arkansas has especial attraction in her unfailing fruits—"fruits large and small never fail, and with this assurance, it will soon become the fruit growers' paradise. It needs no wisdom to forecast the immense fruit trade of Arkansas, whose beginning has surprised the whole country." With the opening up of rail roads north and south, we shall have the advantage of a market north, in Missouri, Kansas, Nebraska and Iowa, for our early fruits; and a market south, for fall and winter fruits. It is well known that south of us fruits are not successfully grown, and at most are a precarious crop. Arkansas is peculiarly a fruit country; her fruits are numerous, consisting of apples, peaches, pears, plums, apricots, cherries, nectarines, grapes, blackberries, strawberries, etc.

This country is the home of the grape, as is demonstrated by the great number and size of the wild grape vines, which permit us to say that grape culture would be most successful. The celebrated muscadine growing here, and many of those wild grapes make good table grapes, and a most excellent quality of wine. It is a fact generally accepted among practical and intelligent fruit growers, that the soil contains the necessary constituents for the successful growing of fruits. In many portions of Arkansas, there are wild grape vines measuring three feet in circumference, and still growing; and those who have planted the grape are more than satisfied with the result. The hilly portions of this State are destined to become vine clad;

soil and climate being highly favorable, equal if not superior to the Herman district in Missouri. The climatic situation is even more favorable than the limestone hills of the Ohio river; the warm, fertile soil and natural drainage, warrant the inference that the growing of fruits would be most successful. The following from the *Real Estate Bulletin*, of Fort Smith, Sebastian county, published by Carnall & Wheeler, men of undoubted integrity, and who have lived in Arkansas over thirty years, and have much practical experience in fruit growing, says: "Contrary to the expectations of the early settlers of this country, it is found to be an excellent climate and soil for fruit generally."

APPLES.

"The trees grow very rapidly on cultivation, too much so. The fall rains grow more wood when the trees are well cultivated, than ripens and becomes firm enough to stand the winters. Of pears, this is especially so, and it is believed to be one cause of the blight in them. As a rule, the winter apples north of 36 deg., though the trees grow as well here as in the north, drop their fruit in August, from the long continued heat of the sun. They will not answer on and south of the Arkansas river.

But we have as great a variety, and equally as fine in quality of southern winter seedlings as can be found in the northern States. We have also, many good summer and fall apples, indigenous to our latitude, though we believe the delicious summer and fall apples of the higher latitudes are, as a rule, equally so here, while the size is much larger. The growth of all fruit trees is much more rapid here than north. We will name some of our best fall and winter apples:

"The Shannon, for fall and early winter, ranks in size and quality with any apple known in the United States."

"The Kentucky Red Streaks, Limber-twig, Ben Davies, Nickajack, Shockley, Prior's Red, Romantie, Stevenson's Winter, Yates, Mangum, Naverick's Sweet, Junaluskee, Chatahooche, Greening, Hall, Webb's Winter and Hughes Crab, are all good varieties for winter, nearly all of them southern seedlings, and are grown and raised here. Summer and fall varieties of fine size and fine quality, are too numerous to mention.

PEACHES.

"The first in ripening here is Hale's Early Ripe, from the first to the fifteenth of June. Fine specimens, this year, 1870, are from six and half to eight inches in circumference and weight, three and a half to five ounces.

Early Crawford comes in from the 10th to 15th July, and is here a most magnificent peach. There are too many fine varieties to enumerate them here. The peach, in this country is a very rapid grower and early bearer; as an instance, a Hale's Early, grafted in February, 1868, and set out in November, 1868, ripened one peach in June, 1869. This is one of the finest peach countries in the world. Plant tansy around the roots to keep off the borer.

PEARS.

"Pears grow to fine size, and in quality will compare favorably with those grown any where, but the trees from very rapid growth, or something else are subject to blight. Much more attention is being paid to them, however, now, than formerly, and many large and delicious varieties are cultivated. The Bartlett, Flemish Beauty, Doucheese D'Angouleme, Winter Nelles and Seekle, are the most noted.

CHERRIES.

"Of cherries, the common Morillo, English Morillo, May Duke, and Graffion or Yellow Spanish, are at present mostly cultivated, but many other kinds are now being tried.

PLUMS.

"All kinds of plums do well here, and there are many wild

kinds all over the country. The most cultivated are the Gages. We saw them this year six inches in circumference. Damson, Coe's Golden Drop, the Wild Goose or Peach, etc.

"Apricots, nectarines, almonds, figs and strawberries, do as well here as any where.

GRAPES.

"As to grapes, we do not think any country, unless it is California, can beat it. Everybody has a vine or so, and several graperies are in cultivation here.

"Every climate and soil has its peculiar fruits and productions; but situated as our country is, and with its varied soil, from the richest alluvial bottoms to its clay sub-soil uplands, with surface from level to rolling, hilly, rocky, and even mountainous, with climate so mild in winter that cattle subsist themselves, we can and do raise almost any fruit, vegetable or farm product that can be raised in the United States, except sugar."

Mr. J. F. McKenzie, on his farm, situated four miles from Fort Smith, in Sebastian county, has a bed of exactly one-tenth of an acre, in Wilson Albany Strawberries, from which, last season, he sold three hundred gallons of strawberries, at from 75 cents to $1 50 per gallon, bringing him the snug sum of about $300 00, besides reserving enough for his own use. This bed was planted in the spring of 1870, and all the cultivation they received was simply to keep out the weeds and grass, and the runners were never cut. The hilly and mountainous portions of the State are of volcanic origin; its soil is similar to the choice wine-producing regions of France, Germany and Italy, with this difference, that the soil of Arkansas is richer, lies better, and easier planted and cultivated. There is no fog, no mist, no long continued damp weather to rot the growing or maturing grape. The latter part of summer when the grape needs the ripening sunbeams, we have the desired weather. Viewed in every respect, I am well satisfied that the hilly regions of this State are singularly well adapted to grape culture, and in fact Arkansas will soon become the great fruit growing State of the Mississippi valley. No crop pays better than a fruit crop, none is surer in this State, neither is there a State in the Union, that has the advantages for remunerative prices in the future; the whole north-west for a market for our early fruit; the whole south for fall and winter; and it is doubtful whether an over supply can be raised; at present there is not half enough fruits raised in the State to supply the home demand, hence none of our fruits find their way to a foreign market. While wealth, under our free civilization, is accumulating and diffusing itself through more numerous classes of society, the demand for fruits will keep pace with any increased production that may be made in this branch of business, and for such crops there is no danger of a failing market, all that part of the country south of 33 deg. north latitude, and that portion north of 42 deg., north latitude can offer but slight competition in the fruit growing business of the United States.

The money product, or an approximation. An acre of ground planted in apple trees, 30 feet apart, will contain say fifty trees, producing each five bushels, at one dollar per bushel the lowest price sold here for, would make $250.

An acre of vineyard, 1,000 vines, producing each ten pounds is 10,000 pounds, at two and a half cents per pound, is $250. Grapes are worth here ten cents, but we give the lowest prices possible. While there is every reason to expect an advance in the value of grapes for wine-making will take place. There are apple trees in Washington county, from which are gathered every year twenty to twenty-five bushels of good sound fruit, which generally brings one dollar and half per bushel. Fruit of all kinds here attain their highest perfection. Strawberries, rasberries, blackberries, whortleberries, plums and delicious grapes are found growing wild in great abundance. Perhaps in no other parts of the country do the wild fruits attain the size and sweetness that they do here, which, in a great measure accounts for the small area devoted as yet to the growing of cultivated fruits. But the building of railroads, which will all be completed before an orchard now planting can come into bearing, rendering the means of distributing the fruit among the hundreds of thousands of eager purchasers, thereby adding greatly to the prices of our fruits, is certainly an inducement for farmers to embark in the general fruit growing business, not only north of the Arkansas river, but in every county south to the Louisiana line; in every county there are localities well adapted to fruit of some kind, and there is no crop more certain or remunerative. Ten years hence there will be found many men in this State, now poor, who made themselves rich by raising and selling fruits on the favored soil of Arkansas.

STOCK RAISING.

Arkansas is especially adapted to stock raising. The soil of the country is covered by luxuriant vegetation of grasses, and both natural and artifical meadows are very fine in the autumnal months, thus furnishing a good and abundant pasture for horses, cattle, and especially sheep; they keep fat on the grass the entire year. Our beef in winter is killed direct from the cane brakes and river bottoms, and make fat, juicy, tender meat, selling at seven cents in summer and ten cents in winter for choice sirloin steaks.

Stock can be bought at the following prices: Horses, from $30 to $125; work mules, from $60 to $150; three year old steers from $12 to $15; yearling, from $3 to $5; milch cows, from $15 to $30. Butter, from twenty cents, in summer, to fifty cents in winter; milk, from forty to eighty cents per gallon, and the supply of milk and butter has never been equal to the home demand. Cheese from twenty-five to thirty-five cents per pound, and we send to Utica, New York, for them, where they are made by farmers upon land worth from $100 to $200 per acre, in a climate requiring four or five months winter feeding. How can they long successfully compete with us? Stock raising and dairying, operating under a sky that demands no shelter, and upon a soil yielding perenial supplies of green food, where land is so cheap that what one acre in New

York would sell for will buy one hundred acres in Arkansas, where crops of grain and grass are almost as certain as the return of the seasons. These are particularly encouraging features to people looking for new homes to come here and locate, and a safe place to embark in new business enterprises. We all know it pays to raise stock in Illinois, where they feed five months out of the twelve. How much more will it pay in Arkansas, where stock can live and thrive the entire year without food or care from the owner, save an occasional salting? But this state of things cannot long exist; our resources need only to be fairly laid before the world, and energetic farmers will come in and possess themselves of these advantages. The forests comprise a great number of nut-bearing trees, and the raising of hogs is a profitable business. Great numbers of them are slaughtered every year, fat from the mast. Pork is worth from five to seven cents per pound, and bacon from twelve to twenty cents per pound.

SHEEP RAISING

Will become a great and profitable business in western and northern Arkansas. The northern States can never compete with Arkansas in sheep raising, for the reason that sheep live from year to year costing absolutely nothing save their salt, and the climate is so mild in winter as to preclude the necessity of shelter. These facts are peculiarly inviting to sheep raisers, and woolen factories will spring up throughout all this country. Ten years hence will see this State, unsurpassed now in natural resources and advantages, teeming with tens of thousands of sheep, whose wool will be manufactured into cloth. Then will her numerous water powers be utilized and made subservient to progressive people; "earnest workers and brains" will convert this State into a rich and powerful empire of itself. The extension of railroad facilities is constantly enlarging the area for stock growing, and with increased facilities for transportation, stock raising will become very profitable, and Arkansas will become one of the great stock raising States of the Mississippi valley. I am satisfied that no country, not even Texas, is comparable to this as a grazing and stock raising region. Cattle and stock generally are healthy, and require no feeding the year round. The rich grass and young cane of the bottoms keep them generally fat enough for beef during the winter months. If it pays to raise stock in Illinois, Iowa or Wisconsin, then the stock raiser should make his fortune in Arkansas.

MINERAL RESOURCES.

Dr. D. D. Owen, late State geologist, says: "Yet, even if no gold should be found profitable to work, there are resources of the State in ores of zinc, manganese, iron, lead and copper, marble, whet and hone stones, rock-crystal, paints, nitre-earths, kaolin, granite, freestone, limestone, marls, green sand, marly limestones, grindstones and slate, which may well justify the assertion that Arkansas is destined to rank as one of the richest mineral States in the Union. Her zinc ores compare very favorably with those of Silesia, and her argentiferous galena far exceeds in per centage of silver, the average of such ores of other countries. Her novaculite rock cannot be excelled in fineness of texture, beauty of color and sharpness of grit. Her crystal mountains stand unrivalled for extent; and their products are equal in brilliancy and transparency to any in the world. The rock-crystal of Montgomery county glitter and flash in the sun's rays, second in brilliancy only to that of the diamond.

MARBLE.

"Immense quarries of marble rock, exhibiting the pink and gray in great perfection, have been opened in various localities, and can be quarried in enormous perfect slabs. Madison county is rich in superior marble quarries.

SLATE.

"Quarries have been opened in Pulaski, Polk, Pike and Sevier counties, of a fine quality, equal if not superior to the best quality of Vermont slate, both as to durability, evenness of of cleaverage, fineness of texture and beauty of color. The application of slate to various purpose are, therefore, now so numerous that good slate quarries are of great importance to a country, as well as to the owners of the property.

"Valuable deposits of

IRON,

"In immense beds, exist throughout the State in many places; and as at Spadra, adjacent to the coal fields, it offers to the iron master great advantages for investment.

"BELLAH LEAD AND SILVER MINES,

"Situated in Sevier county, believed to be an extension of the Kellogg vein, in Pulaski county, gives promise of great productiveness. The argentiferous galena from this mine has been analyzed with the following results: The average yield of lead, 73 per cent. A ton of lead yielded 52½ ounces of silver.

"The northwestern counties contain inexhaustable mines of

LEAD ORES.

"Where the ore has been mined, the lead is represented as lying in pockets, or crevices in the rocks, and not in regular veins. This is the condition in which the ore is also found at the Granby mines in Newton county, Missouri, the richest lead mines in the west, not only from the manner in which the ore occurs in the rocks of Missouri, but it has the same geological horizon, and the same associated minerals. From what is known of this part of the State, there is every reason to believe that valuable deposits of lead ore will be found in the counties of Washington, Benton, Madison, Newton, Carroll, Marion, Searcy, Izard, Independence, Lawrence, and Randolph. A vein of argentiferous galena occurs on Kellogg creek, in Pulaski county."

KAOLIN OR PORCELAIN CLAY.

"The Fourche cove in this county, furnish a fine specimen of kaolin or porcelain clay, derived from the decomposition of felspar.

Noble quarries of granite could be opened on the north slope of the granite range in the Fourche cove. These quarries are only between two and three miles from Little Rock, and close to the line of the Cairo and Fulton rail road. All that is wanted, in order to supply, not only the State of Arkansas, but the whole south and west, with the most substantial of building material, is cheap and easy communication between the quarries and Little Rock."

COAL FIELDS.

"Coal is one of the pride products of Arkansas. Bituminous coal was first discovered and mined near Richmond, Va., in the year 1700, and was extensively used in a foundry, employed in making shot and shell during the revolution in 1775. It was first sent to New York, Boston and Philadelphia in 1789; and the Gore brothers from Connecticut, were the first to make use of anthracite coal in the Wyoming (Pa.,) valley in 1768. Judge Jesse Fell, of Wilkesbarre, was the first to apply it to household uses. Phillip Ginter, a hunter in the Mauch Chunk region, discovered the Lehigh coal in 1791, and in 1812, this coal was sent to Philadelphia.

"Everybody is now acquainted with the general distribution and extent of the great coal basins east of the Mississippi river. The great Appalachian basin occupies part of Pennsylvania, Ohio, Virginia and Kentucky; its western limits being marked by a line running nearly due southward, passing near the mouth of the Scioto river in Ohio. The Illinois coal fields cover parts of Indiana, western Kentucky, Illinois, and throws out spurs into Missouri, Arkansas and further west. The more the spurs are removed from the center of the coal basin, or from its most productive part, the more the coal which they contain becomes valuable, from the scarcity of the combustible mineral. This shows the great value of the coal strata of Arkansas, and the advantage that would result to the State from an extensive and rich coal deposit. Not only the navigation of the Arkansas river would, at a future time, depend upon it, but it would supply with combustible material, the inhabitants of the western prairies, and direct the future construction of rail roads, which are generally attracted by the coal, as by a powerful magnet."

The progress of the civilization of a people, or of a country, is marked by the development of its industry. In this country, the active power of industry is steam. Man is no more a machine, an infant; his mind has subdued matter, has moulded it into the most complicated and diversified forms—has truly animated it—giving it power, strength, indeed life, by the wonderful application of steam. The true generator of steam is coal; thus, a country is more likely to take the lead in industrial development, and therefore in civilization, if it be provided with a large amount of this combustible mineral.

Some of the most celebrated geographers and philosophers of our time have asserted, that the continent of North America, and especially the great valley of the Mississippi would, at a future day, become inhabited by the densest and most civilized population of the world, because it has, in its extensive coal fields, the largest amount of coal, that originator of industrial life.

ARKANSAS COAL FIELDS.

"Arkansas contains 12000 square miles of coal. Coal has already been found and surveyed in twelve counties. The combustible mineral is rendered more valuable, because the coal basin is situated along the Arkansas river, and on both sides of it. Washington, Crawford, Sebastian, Franklin, Scott, Johnson, Yell, Pope, Perry, Conway, White and Pulaski counties, are all of them, almost entirely, situated in the coal basin of Arkansas; and its productive strata may yet be extended into some of the adjacent counties, when the combustible mineral shall become valuable enough to encourage explorations by boring. The value of the coal beds of a country is necessarily relative, and cannot be estimated by comparison with the price or value of coal at another place. A bed of bituminous coal, four feet thick, is remunerative when worked along the Ohio river; although, from an excessive competition, the coal is sometimes delivered to boats at five cents per bushel."

"IN ARKANSAS,

"Where the coal is semi-bituminous, or half anthracite, and consequently of higher value as a heating agent than the bituminous coal of the east, where also this combustible material, though still uncalled for by manufactures, is sold at the bank at from ten to fifteen cents per bushel, the coal has a much higher value. From data collected in statistical tables, it results that a coal vein like the Spadra's, three and a half feet thick, producing about three feet of clear coal, will hereafter and when the coal becomes more pressing, give to the owners more profitable results than a bank of nine feet of anthracite coal would give in the central part of Pennsylvania."

Our mines are worked in the old fashioned way—by main strength. The strippings are from three to thirteen feet, and the veins from three to nine feet thick. And it should be remembered that this comprises the upper coal measure, leaving the middle and lower to be yet explored. Only here and there are the beds of coal being worked, for the reason that the supply has been much greater than the demand. What a change is soon to take place; when our railroads are completed, the coal which is now almost valueless, and coal lands which even now can be bought very cheap, will be worth many hundred dollars per acre. What, then, will be the profits of mining when steam power is used for hoisting and pumping? At present every shower drowns out the miners.

Energetic northern men have already turned their attention to the great mineral wealth of this State. It is a peculiarity of the mineral lands of this State, that no fictitious value has been placed on them. Adjacent to our mineral lands are some of the finest farming lands in the State, only awaiting the hand of the husbandman to make them bloom and productive of their golden harvest. It is a surprising fact a region so wonderful rich in mineral wealth should have been left unproductive until now. The only conclusion I can arrive at is that the peculiar institution of the south, before the war, prevented capitalists and free labor from investing in or coming to the south, and it is only in the last two or three years that our rich mineral wealth has become known to the outside world. Yet Arkansas is a young State only in her infancy, and her mineral resources are just beginning to be developed. What may we expect when they are freely developed? But these facts teach us what a great State she will be. These resources are availably located; they are developed by navigable rivers, and soon will be traversed by railroads through all parts of the State; their value is incalculable, their extent boundless and their richness unequaled.

"The following is a chemical analysis of a specimen taken from the upper member of a five foot vein, at Green's bank, in Sebastian county:

Volatile matter	13.75	Water	1.40
		Gas	12.35
		Fixed carbon	82.25
Coke	86.25	Ashes, flesh color	4.00
			100.00

This coal swells up considerably in coking. The analysis proves this coal to be semi-bituminous, and far richer in fixed carbon than most of the coal in the western States, and therefore, of course, twice as durable in the fire, with proper access of air. It contains just enough volatile combustible matter to keep it ignited without the artificial blast required for anthracite."

There are in Sebastian county veins of coal nine feet in thickness, at a depth of twenty feet, lying idle because there is as yet not sufficient demand to justify the owners buying engines and pumps necessary to work them, and coal lands are held at no higher price than ordinary agricultural lands. But parties from the east and from Europe are making inquiries respecting mineral lands, and the prospects are that a large amount of capital will be invested in mineral lands, and in a majority of cases by men who intend to develop the property at once.

LIGNITES.

"In the south-eastern part of the State, there are extensive beds of lignites, which will become valuable in the future, especially for the use of steamboats in the navigation of the rivers."

SALT.

"Salt springs have been worked for years in Dallas and Hot Spring counties, and there is every reason to believe that an abundant supply of brine may be obtained on boring deeper."

HOT SPRINGS.

The Hot Springs of Arkansas, noted throughout the United States for their curative qualities, are situated about sixty miles south-west from Little Rock. "Their number is fifty-four, and some of them are hot enough to cook an egg; those that are mostly used for bathing, have a temperature at the fountain head of 148 deg. Fahrenheit's thermometer, the waters of which, after being conducted in open troughs down the hill side, to the reservoirs above the bath houses, and standing some time, are just as hot as the skin can bear. If then, the Warm Springs of Virginia, which have a temperature of only 96 to 98 deg., exercise, as experience has proved, a most potent effect in the cure of many diseases, "mainly by their temperature," how much more positive must be the effect of waters of so much higher temperature? especially when a stream of it, in diameter as large as a man's arm, can be directed at pleasure, with great force on any organ. In many forms of chronic diseases, especially, its effects are truly astonishing, and indeed powerful, arousing into action sluggish and torpid secretions; the languid circulation is thus purified of morbific matters, and thereby renewed vigor and healthful action are given, both to the absorbents lymphatics, and to the execretion apparatus—a combined effect which no medicine is capable of accomplishing."

The late Dr. D. D. Owen, State Geologist, "attributes the high temperature of these waters to the internal heat of the earth. Not that the waters come in actual contact with fire, but rather, that the waters are completely permeated with highly heated vapors and gasses, which emanate from sources deeper seated than the water itself."

The Hon. James Hinds, in his speech of July 25th, 1868, in the United States House of Representatives, said: "These springs are fifty-four in number; having a temperature varying from 93 to 150 degrees Farenheit, and discharge 317 gallons per minute. The amount discharged from each varies, but they are all qualitively allied. It is estimated by eminent medical gentlemen, that there are over 100,000 afflicted persons in the United States, who cannot be permanently cured, except by the use of these waters; and the day is not far distant when a great city will rise on the mountain slope, which will be the Baden-Baden of America."

Dr. Lawrence, a resident physician says: "The properties of these waters depend not alone on their caloric qualities, but the springs all contain carbonates of the alkalies, and alkaline earth, agents well known to therapeutists to possess an active eliminative agency; consequently they produce valuable alterative effects in chronic diseases. Rheumatism, gout, stiff joints, contraction of the muscles and skin, old wounds and painful cicatrices, are relieved; skin diseases, scrofulous ulcerations, and enlargement of the glands, prostrations from long standing sickness, or debility following severe courses of powerful medicines, show a remarkable improvement; spinal diseases, neuralgia, nervous affections, partial paralysis, lead palsey, St. Vitus dance, muscular and general debility respond to the treatment. Uterine diseases, as a class, are greatly benefitted, and the baths here particularly regarded for the grand climacteric change of life. For mercurial diseases, volumes of testimonials could be adduced in relation to the effects of these remarkable and unexcelled waters."

"It is believed that, in the cure of diseases, there are no springs in the world, that can compare with the Hot Springs of Arkansas."—*Homes in Arkansas.*

THE MAMMOTH SPRING.

"In Fulton county is a remarkable phenomenon, its waters either by compression, or from some other peculiar cause, contains apparently, in solution, such a great amount of carbonic acid, that its surface is in a continuous state of effervesence or bubbling, resembling the effervesence of a fountain of soda water. The constant temperature of the water, 60 degrees, favors apparently, the development of animal life; and the number of species of water plants growing near the borders, but still in the waters, such as Indian rice, water cress, marsh speedwell, etc., is the cause of allurement for fowls, especially during the winter months. This place will, doubtless in the future, acquire great importance as affording a healthy and pleasant place of summer resort."

The main body of water issues from a large cavernous opening, forty yards in circumference, and boils up with a constant flow, at the rate of 8000 barrels per minute. It affords valuable water power for general manufacturing purposes.

MANUFACTURES.

"No great community, living in a fertile and productive country, can be long or largely prosperous unless it shows a certain amount of independence, or rather an ability and disposition to supply most of its ordinary wants." The example of England and Germany conclusively shows that the nation or State, that utilizes its forces, and encourages the employment of every human faculty, is the one which becomes the most powerful and rich; whilst the example of Persia and Turkey, shows that the nations that engage in one pursuit, to the comparative neglect of all others, do not have a flourishing growth, and are not capable of resisting adversity. The people of a State should so direct their employments, that success would not be contingent upon a bountiful harvest from a single crop. They should establish and stimulate manufactures, open and develop mines and diversify their avocations. Before the war, the southern States, by directing all their energies to the production of cotton and sugar, and neglecting the grain crops, had to look to the north almost entirely for their breadstuffs. But since the war they have learned to produce a large portion of their food supplies, and, as a result, will soon be more prosperous than ever before. Enterprise and industry, moved by the hand of capital, and guided by the skill and ingenuity of the miner and manufacturer, is what has built up the north. Here we have all the elements necessary to maintain manufacturing towns, all through the State. And those who are favored by land and country, so as to be able to organize; the producer and consumer, side by side; the farmer, mechanic, miner and manufacturer, are all beneficial to each other, for the reason that each wants the products of the other in exchange for his own, and thus creates a market for all, thereby stimulating industry, hence the advantage to be derived from a diversified industry.

Arkansas has abundant water power, extensive coal fields, cheap labor, and illimitable quantities of the raw material, entering into the thousand manufactured products suited to the wants of a civilized people. If it will but put forth its hand it can successfully compete with either "New England or Old England" in the manufacture of many articles, to procure which, it now sends its money abroad. Valuable forests of the best timber used in mechanical industry are to be found all over the State, and will, in due time, furnish material for agricultural implements, furniture, and the various uses to which timber is employed. In all parts of the State are valuable mines of metals and minerals. What more favorable place, for effecting a junction of the raw material, with the consumers, without the cost of long transportation. There is probably no better unoccupied field in the United States, for manufactories, cotton and woolen mills should be built here, when the raw material and consumer are brought in close contact, thereby being mutually beneficial to the manufacturer and consumer. Where all the raw materials are convenient, abundant and cheap, and where profitable establishments can be built up at once to supply the rapidly increasing demands. The State laws are as favorable as could be asked for the manufacturer. The Legislature, at its last session, passed a bill entitled "An act for the encouragement of domestic industry, approved March 28, 1871:"

SECTION 1. "The collection of all taxes payable into the treasury of the State, or of any county or municipal organization in the State, upon capital stock, premises, machinery, and all tools, materials or other property, directly pertaining to the conduct of such manufacturing or mining business, together with the products of such manufactory or mine, while in the ownership and possession of the original manufacturer or miner, shall be, and is hereby suspended for the term of five years, after the first collection of taxes on real estate, following the date of the passage of this act."

By diversifying our crops, and multiplying our avocations, make all our provisions, manufacture all our agricultural implements and hundreds of articles, that is now draining us of our money. "Build up manufacturing towns, make our own clothing, and every thing possible, to supply our wants at home; this policy adopted will make the people of Arkansas prosperous, powerful and wealthy; this state of things will as surely result as effects follow their legitimate causes." And we hesitate not to say that within the next ten years, there are to be wonderful developments of the great resources of this State. We have a good country and desire a million progressive, intelligent and energetic emigrants to come in, aid and assist in developing the country and share the benefits to be derived therefrom.

VALUE OF LANDS IN ARKANSAS.

Land, of itself considered, has comparative little value; it is the labor and capital expended upon it, directly and indirectly, that gives it value; roads, railroads, cities, churches and school houses, all add to the value of land. Arkansas offers to the immigrant advantages superior to most all other States; it has but a small population as yet, and consequently workers with capital are few. In the north, where laborers are plenty, all want land, and of course land goes up. The lands of Arkansas, under the new order of things, will advance in price rapidly, because of the great number of navigable rivers adjacent thereto. It is a demonstrated fact, that lands lying contiguous to large rivers will enhance to a greater value by reason of the lasting and cheap transit afforded.

Capitalists and others seeking land investments are turning their attention to the rich lands of Arkansas, the value of which will be greatly enhanced by the building of the now projected railroads. Nothing is more certain than the rapid increase in the price of lands in Arkansas, and immigrants should come in and secure to themselves homes while land is cheap. There is now hardly a man in middle life and moderate circumstances, who might not be wealthy to-day, had he only been able to foresee twenty years ago the astonishing rise in real estate in various parts of the country; but he did not foresee, did not buy and have confidence in the future. The same chances are offered now; a greater rise will take place in the next twenty years than the last twenty. There is not a section of land in this State, though ever so far from a railroad or river now, but what will be worth in twenty years from $30 to $50 per acre. Lands on a lease, rent or sale can be obtained upon various terms. Improved lands can be leased for a term of years upon the payment of taxes and a small rent; or can be bought and the price paid each year in crops if desired. Any farm here, well worked, will soon pay for itself. Improved farms are worth all the way from $5 to $50 per acre, depending upon the quality of soil, improvements, access to markets, etc.; unimproved land, from 50 cents to $30 per acre, and the same will produce one bale to a bale and a half, or forty to sixty bushels of corn to the acre. Land owners will cut up their farms into forty or eighty acre tracts and allow buyers their own time on most of the payments, with proper legal protection.

It is erroneous to say that white labor cannot raise cotton. White labor has and is now successfully raising cotton; all the children can be efficiently employed in hoeing and picking. "The energetic farmer can here attain the competence for which he would have long to labor in vain upon the cold bleak plains of the north or sterile soil of the east." Here are fertile farms, with water, wood, etc., which in some instances can be purchased at lower figures than the original cost of the improvements upon the same. There are about fifteen million acres of land which can be taken up under the homestead law. In the northern and western portions of the State there are millions of acres of the finest fruit lands in the Union, which can be bought for from fifty cents to five dollars per acre.

In the extreme eastern portion of the State there is an immense body of the richest land in the world, which can be reclaimed by drainage, and that, too, at a moderate cost, compared with the value of the land when redeemed. "The comparison of the agricultural products of the reclaimed soil with that of the dry alluvial upland is full evidence of the value of the drainage of the low lands." Not only can a large portion of the land in the northern and western portions of the State be obtained very cheaply, but even finely cultivated farms along the valleys of the Arkansas, Ouachita, White and other rivers can be purchased lower than the same kind of land and improvements in Missouri or Illinois. No State offers stronger inducements to the enterprising and industrious immigrant than Arkansas. If he wants cotton, grain, grass or fruit land he can get it at a cheap rate; or if he is a miner, work is plenty, pay is good, society is good, the people are as law abiding and moral as anywhere. The inhabitants comprise people from all the States. The fertility of the soil, reasonableness in price of lands, healthfulness of climate, and soon to be near access to markets and the great centers of commerce, present advantages to the immigrant that can be afforded nowhere else. The lands of this State are far preferable to the low priced lands of the northwest, on account of the greater variety of products and comparative immunity from drouths; and further because the farmer has twice as long time to prepare the land and plant his crop, and when the crops are gathered, the cost of transportation to market will be less because nearer and free from ice blockades.

GOVERNMENT LANDS.

All male persons and unmarried females, of lawful age, are entitled under the laws of the government to a homestead and pre-emption of land, consisting of one hundred and sixty acres each, or three hundred and twenty acres in the aggregate. The homestead costs nothing, save the fees, amounting to $18 for 160 acres; $9 for 80 acres; $7 for forty acres; 20 per cent. of the above amounts can be reserved until the expiration of five years, at which time the settler gets his patent from the government; the title being secured by an actual residence of five years upon the land. The pre-emption of one hundred and sixty acres costs $1 25 per acre, and a few dollars more for fees. Thus a man can secure his homestead of 160 acres at a cost of $18, and he then has the privilege of entering 160 acres more, and the whole 320 acres will cost him only some $250. This is extremely liberal on the part of the government, and is all that can be desired on the part of the settler. It must be remembered that the land thus secured in Arkansas, is as fine as any in the world for the production of grain, fruits, vegetables or stock raising.

Persons desiring to get government land, should select their locality, go to the district land office and get plats made of a few townships, then with these go out and get some settler to help you look out a piece to suit you; you then can go to the office and make your entry, after which, if a homestead, you are allowed six months in which to establish your home upon the land, and no one can interfere with your entry during that time.

There are seven land offices in the State:

No. 1. Batesville District, at Batesville, Independence county.

No. 2. Fayetteville District, at Huntsville, Madison county.

No. 3. Clarksville District, at Dardanelle, in Pope county.

No. 4. Little Rock District, at Little Rock, Pulaski county.

No. 5. Helena District, at Helena, in Phillips county.

No. 6. Washita District, at Champagnolle, in Union county.

No. 8. Washington District, at Washington, in Hempstead county.

Then, in addition to the government lands, the State has several hundred thousand acres of land forfeited to the State for taxes, which she gives to settlers free of cost, only requiring improving and occupation to perfect the title to the same to the settler. These are called, "State Donation or Forfeited Lands." We give the laws of the State in relation to these lands:

Sec. 2. "The right of the State to all lands which have, and all which at a future period will, have been forfeited for taxes, and not redeemed nor sold, may be donated to actual settlers, or such persons as will become settlers thereon, or improve the land as required by this act.

"Sec. 4. Any person wishing to obtain such donation, should apply to the auditor of public accounts of the State, who shall execute under his hand and official seal, a deed, conveying all the right, title and interest of the State thereto, conditioned that the party receiving such donation shall reside upon and improve and cultivate at least three acres, or instead of residing on said tract shall within eighteen months, clear, fence and improve five acres.

"Sec. 12. Every head of a family shall be entitled to take up a quarter section of land, subject to donation, in his or her own name, by complying with the provisions of the law above stated.

"Sec. 13. Every male head of a family shall also be entitled to take up a quarter section of said donation lands, in the name of his wife and each of his minor children, and the deed shall be made to them respectively, but the improvements required to be made by existing laws, as a condition of title, shall be dispensed with as to the land taken up in the name of the wife and minor heirs."

"SEC. 16. Any head of a family, who shall apply for donation lands, in the name of their minor children, shall make and subscribe an affidavit that they are bona fide citizens of the State.

"SEC. 5. Each individual, receiving such donation, shall, upon completing the improvements required to be made upon the land deeded to him, obtain from such justice of the peace, residing in the township where said land is situated, a certificate setting forth the quarter section, township, range and county, where said land is situated, which certificate shall be attested by the justice and filed in the auditor's office, and such certificate shall be evidence that the donee has complied with that part of the law requiring the land to be improved."

RAIL ROAD LANDS.

Immigrants will often find it to their advantage to buy land of the railroad companies, thereby securing the benefit of long time and easy payments, which will enable them to use their cash for improvements, buy stock, tools, etc. Good railroad lands can be bought for from two to twenty-five dollars per acre, in as good a country as the sun shines on. "Nature could do, and man could ask but very little more." Good soil, good timber, plenty of coal, an abundance of building stone, water, etc., and that within easy reach of towns, rivers and railroads.

We have a fine country, fine climate and reproductive soil; but let no one come here thinking he can make a living farming without work; this is the best lazy man's country I ever saw, but enterprise and industry is no where better rewarded. We want energetic and industrious farmers, and such will soon acquire a competency; patience and industry being the heavier portion of the capital required.

The Memphis and Little Rock railroad have 150,000 acres of

fine land along the line of the road, which is offered at greatly reduced prices. Great inducements will be offered to actual settlers who will improve the land.

The Little Rock and Fort Smith railroad company have 1,000,000 acres of choice river, creek bottom and upland, for sale on credit, or for cash, at low rates. These lands are in alternate sections, on each side and within twenty miles of the line of the road.

The Iron Mountain and Helena railroad company have a large tract of as fine lands as can be found in that portion of the State, situated on each side of the road from the Missouri line to Helena; land that will grow grain, grass or fruit equal to the lands of any State.

The Cairo and Fulton rail road company have a munificent land grant of 301 miles long, by 40 miles wide, embracing 1,800,000 acres of as fine land as can be found west of the Mississippi river, being alternate sections on each side of the line of the road, from the north-east portion of the State, to the extreme south-west portion. And the road being located along that portion of the country, where the hilly regions of western and northern Arkansas meets the level lands of the eastern and southern portions of the State, enables the Cairo and Fulton rail road to satisfy the wants of all classes of buyers, either for bottom, valley, or hilly lands; for cotton, grain, fruit or stock growing. The country through which the Cairo and Fulton rail road runs, is equally as rich as the celebrated blue grass region of Kentucky, with a climate far more preferable. Why, the country is not known. What a land this will be when the Cairo and Fulton rail road sends daily trains thundering along through these splendid lands. Fifty dollars per acre will be the value of these lands then, which can be bought now for from $2 00 to $10 00 per acre on long time.

The object of the company is to sell these lands very low to actual settlers, and thereby rapidly fill up the country along the line of their road, with an industrious and thrifty people, whose wants in the future will remunerate the company in freights; and whose products of the soil will help to sustain the local traffic of the road. It is short sighted policy for any company to hold their lands at high figures. Better to give the land to actual settlers, than hold on for years to receive a big price for the land, and at the same time run the road through a barren country.

The Cairo and Fulton rail road company look at this matter in the true light, and are determined to fill up the country along the line of their road, by the time the trains get fairly started for the through trip.

The Mississippi, Ouachita and Red River rail road, have a large grant of land for sale, located on both sides and within twenty miles of the line of the road. These lands are covered with forests of some of the finest pine and oak timber in the Union, and naturally suggest to the mind the immense lumber business that will grow up here when the rail road is completed, finding a remunerative market at New Orleans, and places up the river.

In an agricultural point, the land through which the road runs, is one of the richest cotton and corn countries in the State, yielding, annually, immense crops of those articles, which is a strong inducement for the rapid completion of the road; and still a stronger inducement for settlers to secure to themselves a home, at low figures and on long terms, along the line of the Mississippi, Ouachita and Red River rail road. From the very nature of things these lands are soon to become very valuable.

The Little Rock, Pine Bluff and New Orleans rail road company have a large land grant, of some as fine lands as Arkansas boasts of within her borders. These lands were contributed by parties along the line of the road as local aid, and a valuable aid they will be ten years hence to the fortunate owners. Land that will bring one bale of cotton, or 50 to 75 bushels of corn to the acre, will then bring an annual rent of ten dollars per acre. A hundred acres, costing now about one thousand dollars, would then bring one thousand dollars, annually, in rents, to say nothing of the increase in value on the purchase price. Truly the outside world are ignorant of the lands of this State, and the natural advantages we possess. But we have now opened our ports, and give an invitation to all desiring to become actual settlers, that we offer inducements equaled by no other State.

Almost every rail road company in the State, have more or less lands for sale, which have been acquired by United States, State, county or individul grant, to aid said enterprise. The granting of land to rail road companies, was first conceived by Stephen A. Douglas, to induce the building of the Illinois Central rail road, through the unbroken prairies of Illinois. That company received large franchises in land. The work commenced, and settlements flooded those hitherto tenantless prairies; and now the wide wild waste of prairie teems and blossoms with fertility and productiveness. Land grants to rail roads are a great incentive to rapid settlement, and at the same time valuable aid to the rail road companies. Take a grant of one million acres, sold at ten dollars per acre, realizing ten million dollars; that sum will build and equip two hundred miles of rail road in this State.

CREDIT OF ARKANSAS.

A country possessing such vast stores of mineral wealth, and containing such an immense body of rich and productive lands, covered with vast forests of the finest timber in the world, although much of it is still undeveloped and unproductive, "should have proper credit and consideration in all the bureaus of finance throughout the world; should have her bonds as good as gold." They are rapidly advancing now, and we may confidently soon expect them to be at par in spite of the heavy Real Estate bank debt incurred before the war. Arkansas, by a constitutional provision submitted to and duly ratified by the people, funded her old debt and the accrued interest thereon into new bonds, payable in thirty years, with interest at the rate of six per cent. per annum. This debt is being canceled, and very soon Arkansas sixes will stand at par.

Hon. Henry Page, State Treasurer, in his report, says: "The punctual payment of the interest which is paid semi-annually, is secured by a special tax of one-fourth of one per cent. upon the entire taxable property of the State, the assessed value of which will approximate to $120,000,000. The entire amount of new bonds issued up to the 1st day of March, 1871, in redemption of the old debt is $2,750,000, which, together with the amount outstanding and unredeemed, the largest portion of which is now held by the government for account of the Smithsonian Institute, will make the actual debt about $4,430,-000. But this debt, small as it is for a State of such large resources, and which raised last year 300,000 bales of cotton, netting the planters a little less than $20,000,000, will be gradually diminished by the proceeds of sales of real estate held by the State under the bank mortgages. From these mortgages, which are now in process of foreclosure, it is estimated there will be realized nearly $3,000,000, and the proceeds are expressly set apart by a constitutional provision to be applied to the extinguishment of the State indebtedness."

Assessed value of real estate in 1860		$ 63,254,740
Entire taxable property in 1870, nearly		120,000,000
No. acres improved land in 1860	1,933,036	
No. acres improved land in 1870	2,340,687	
Cash value of farms in 1860		$91,673,403
Cash value of farms in 1870		80,000,000
Cash value of implements and machinery in 1860		4,024,114
Cash vlaue of animals in 1860		22,040,211
Cash value of implements and machinery in 1870		5,642,391
Cash value of animals in 1870		25,290,397
No. of 400 lb. cotton bales in 1860		367,485
No. of 450 lb. cotton bales in 1870		300,000

When it is remembered that the whole State of Arkansas does not contain but 485,000 inhabitants, the above showing is highly creditable.

"The taxes for the past year realized about one million dollars, being nine and a half mills to the dollar upon the taxable property of the State, taken at a very low rate of assessment. To-day Arkansas is punctually meeting all her engagements; paying the interest upon her debt as promptly as any of the older States. Nor should it be forgotten that eighty millions of taxable values, the value of slave property in the State, were swept away by the war."

EDUCATION.

Let us pass from the great and varied resources of the State "to some of the details which constitute the grand result. When we speak of the wealth of the State, we should not so much consider its rich mines, its fruitful soil, its salubrious climate, and its natural channels of commerce, as its people. The people are all that give real wealth to any country. Without inhabitants, the fairest lands upon which the sun shines would be of no more value than a barren beach or rocky cliff. But then, the people must have intelligence in order to give value to a country they inhabit. Savages make a land poorer instead of richer by their presence. And just in proportion as a community rise in the scale of civilization, intelligence, refinement and moral worth, their lands and houses go up in their money value."

The public schools of Arkansas are ample to secure to all classes the fullest opportunities to acquire an education, and have a thoroughness and efficiency not surpassed by those of Massachusetts. Seventy-two sections, 46,080 acres, of land was given by the United States to this State for a public seminary. The saline lands in the State, not to exceed 46,080 acres, go to the school fund; section sixteen in every township belongs to the school fund of the State; all taxes collected from the sixteenth section, after being sold, go into the school fund; the proceeds of all property escheated to the State go into the school fund; all moneys derived from posting estrays, and a portion of the sales of forfeited lands, go into the school fund; and finally, one dollar per capita tax, to be annually assessed on every male inhabitant over twenty-one years of age, goes into the school fund. Thus, you will see, Arkansas has a good and permanent school fund to secure to all classes the benefits of an education.

The teachers receive here from sixty to one hundred, averaging about eighty, dollars per month. The school buildings and the opportunities afforded for education may very justly be taken as a fair criterion from which to form a judgment of a country's prosperity The general intelligence of the community at large is of itself sufficient evidence of the facilities for improvement and information afforded them.

The constitution of the State provides that "the General Assembly shall require by law that every child of sufficient mental and physical ability, shall attend the public school during the period between the ages of five and eighteen years, for a term equivalent to three years, unless educated by other means." The law also provides that the white and colored children shall be educated in separate schools.

NAVIGABLE STREAMS.

While in other States, until supplied with railroads, farmers were obliged to haul their products, in many instances, two hundred miles to a market, in this State the water courses are so distributed that almost every portion of the State has water facilities for transportation to market. No other State in the Union equals Arkansas in this respect.

1. The Mississippi river forms the eastern boundary of the State, with its bends, make a border of about 400 miles, affording steamboat facilities to the counties of Chicot, Desha, Phillips, Crittenden and Mississippi.

2. The Arkansas river rises in Middle Park, Colorado, and after receiving the tributaries for 1200 miles, enters the western border of the State at Fort Smith, running through the State south-east for 600 miles, affording steamboat navigation its whole course through to the following counties: Desha, Arkansas, Jefferson, Pulaski, Conway, Perry, Pope, Yell, Johnson, Franklin, Crawford and Sebastian.

3. The Ouachita river rises in Polk county, and affords steam navigation to Arkadelphia, 200 miles, furnishing transportation for Ashley, Union, Calhoun, Ouachita, Dallas, Clark and Montgomery counties.

4. The White river is navigable to Batesville, 400 miles, and during high water 100 miles further, affording facilities for shipment to Desha, Arkansas, Monroe, Woodruff, White, Jackson and Independence counties.

5. The Saint Francis river is navigable to the Missouri line, through the counties of Phillips, Saint Francis, Crittenden, Cross, Mississippi, Poinsett, Craighead and Green.

6. Black river is navigable 200 miles, affording water facilities to Jackson, Independence, Lawrence, Green and Randolph counties.

7. Saline river is navigable about 100 miles, running through the counties of Hot Springs, Dallas, Jefferson, Bradley, Drew, Ashley and Calhoun.

8. Red river, running through the south-western portion of the State, is navigable in the counties through which it passes, viz: Little River, Hempstead and Lafayette; a distance of about 100 miles.

9. Bayou Bartholomew empties into the Ouachita river, and is navigable, in this State, about 150 miles, affording steamboat facilities to Ashley, Chicot, Drew and Desha counties.

Of the sixty-one counties in the State, forty-three are watered by streams, each navigable, affording to Arkansas more than twenty-five hundred miles of water highway, and it must be remembered that the ice king never obstructs navigation in the State of Arkansas.

Besides these navigable streams there are a great many smaller tributaries, which will, when the country is older and wealthier, be converted into canals and water powers, and thus furnish, not only transit but motive power, to convert the raw material into the wants of man. The creeks and their numerous affluents, constitute a system of drainage and water works for supplying man and beast with nature's healthful beverage, and nourish along their banks forests of cedar and pine, mines of iron and coal, and furnish in their clear, pure waters the favorite haunts of the numerous finny tribe known to abound in those streams.

TIMBER.

No State in the west is better supplied with an abundance of valuable timber than Arkansas. Here is timber enough to supply all the factories of the United States for years. The number and species of timber in these forests are numerous and great, consisting of yellow pine, poplar, black walnut, cherry, sugar maple, beech, honey-locust, red, black, white and post-oak, cypress, red elm, sycamore, cotton wood, hickory, gum, ash, buckeye, laurel, shingle oak, in fact every variety of timber used in the mechanical arts. (The under growth consist of elder, pawpaw, spice wood, hazel, cane and grape vines;) and yet scarcely a factory for manufacturing timber into the various uses to which it is employed, in the State. This state of things wont long exist. In addition to our wants are the long, lank arms of the timberless regions of the west, stretched out for supplies. Then, in addition to this are the hucksters and runners, that swarm through the land in search of ship-timber, car-timber, cabinet-timber, pipe, butt, oil and barrel-staves. Besides this, the demand for timber to build our steamers, sail and other vessels; docks and elevators for our vast inland waters, and the requirements to build our cities, villages, farm buildings, and to bridge our streams, fence our fields, and the thousand other unnamed uses to which timber is daily applied, gives but a faint idea of the demand for lumber and timber to-day. But who shall compute the demand in the future? Every cough from the locomotives' hoarse lungs augments it. The statistics of the lumber business in the United States, though by no means full or perfect, show a ratio of increase, since 1867, beyond all precedence in the past. It has become an interest of immense magnitude. Will it continue to increase in the same proportions? The future will determine the question. To every appearance it will. The question of future supplies, the limit of value that will be reached, as well as the value of timber lands, may well be studied. Trees do not grow in a day, and as a general rule, when they are cut down, so much timber is forever used up. The intrinsic value of timber, the relative value of the different kinds, the near day in the future that will see the pine and other forests of the north-west exhausted, with the accumulating agencies of destruction now at work, will divert the attention of the capitalist, manufacturer and dealer in lumber and timber, to the especial attractions of Arkansas. Surely the outside world cannot be aware of the resources of this fine country, or there would be manifested a deeper interest in the means of developing it. Cord wood, delivered in the various towns, is worth from $2 50 to $5 00 per cord; walnut and other lumber, for making furniture, is worth, delivered, from fifteen to thirty dollars per thousand; and yet we send to Cincinnati, where the same quality of lumber is worth sixty-five dollars per thousand, for all our furniture; pine lumber, from fifteen to twenty five dollars per thousand, and all other kinds at an equally cheap rate. Who will contend that such an outrage upon the law of trade can long exist? And the attention of capitalists and manufacturers need only be fairly attracted to this State, where the elements exist, to take advantage of them at once.

What more favorable place in the country for effecting a junction of the raw material with the consumers, without the cost of transportation? What a field is open to them; a country destitute of even a furniture factory, and where the demand is daily increasing. "Not a plow factory, and iron, coal and wood abounding, merely awaiting the skill of the manufacturer to turn it immediately into implements of all kinds, so greatly needed." Here should be work-shops for making wagons, carriages, axe-helves, hoop-poles, fork, hoe, rake, and broom handles, and in fact all articles that can be made of wood; the difference in the cost of freight making a handsome profit, and inducement for the building of manufactories in this State, which cannot long be overlooked by capital and the enterprising people of the country.

RAIL ROADS.

"To determine the importance of a State or city, its essential condition and advantages must be defined and understood, both in their immediate and approximate relations; and to ascertain their future greatness and controlling influence, their local and general relations must be understood and considered in connection with the natural advantages which they possess, for the civil and industrial pursuits of man; and their natural and artificial facilities for the exchange of the products of different lands and climates, and the intercommunication of one people with another. The most important consideration of the subject, is her system of rail roads."

The immense State of Arkansas, of inexhaustible agricultural and mineral resources, will be rapidly filled with population; its productions of cotton, corn, wheat, etc., are daily increasing, and its rail road wants are rapidly growing. The rail roads that are now building in the State, will create a new Arkansas out of *old* Arkansas; they will attract capital and labor to this thinly settled and undeveloped country. The entire State of Arkansas, in a few years, will be checkered over her entire domain with rail roads. It is a great State, and when immigrants flow in to increase her population and wealth, she will be a wonderful State.

In 1860, Arkansas had but 38½ miles of completed rail road. In 1870 there was 128 miles of operated rail road in the State. One mile of rail road to every 407¾ square miles, and one mile to every 3,906 inhabitants.

"In 1868 an Act was submitted to, and ratified by the people, granting State aid to the extent of $15,000 per mile, to roads having no land grants; and $10,000 per mile to those with such a grant, to the extent of 850 miles." This aid has been awarded to the following roads:

Name.	Length of Miles.	Awarded.	Issued.	Completed.
M. & L. R. R. R.	131	$1,200,000	$1,200,000	131 miles.
Little Rock and F. S. R R.	150	1,500,000	900,000	50..do..
L. R. P. B. & N. O. R. R.	160	2,400,000	750,000	20..do..
M. O. & Red River R. R.	170	2,540,000	450,000	42..do..
Arkansas Central R. R.	150	2,250,000	300,000	40..do..
Kansas City & F. S. R. R.	100	1,500,000	....	....
Total	850	$11,400,000	$3,600,000	....

These bonds run thirty years, and draw six per cent interest. The rail road companies are required to pay the interest.

Prior to this law, Arkansas had only 48 miles of operated rail road. By the terms of the law, State bonds can be issued to rail road companies, as sections of ten miles are graded and prepared for rails, while a rigid showing may be required of the uses to which the bonds previously issued have been put. Up to this time the interest has been promptly paid by all the roads to whom bonds have been issued.

The cost of building rail roads in Arkansas, as compared with other States, are very favorable, and as follows:

States.	Miles of R. R.	Population.	Cost per mile.
Arkansas	128	485,000	$43,562
Texas	583	750,000	36,044
Louisiana	375	730.000	40,577
Kansas	1,150	600,000	40,540
Missouri	1.800	1,600,000	54,995
Iowa	2,095	1,250,000	39,407
Illinois	4,036	2,567,532	42,791
West Virginia	387	400,000	68,498
Pennsylvania	4,898	3,500,000	52,037
New York	3,658	4,400,000	50,431
Massachusetts	1,480	1,350,000	59,704

We now procced to set forth, in part, the rail road system of the State:

1. Memphis and Little Rock Rail Road.—From Memphis, Tennessee, to Little Rock, length 131 miles, completed and in operation, doing a large and paying business.

2. Little Rock and Fort Smith Rail Road.—From Little Rock to the western part of the State, at Fort Smith; 50 miles in operation, 60 more graded and about ready for the ties and iron; and balance, 40 miles, have been some work done on a portion. This road will be pushed to completion the present year, under the management of the new directors.

3. Little Rock, Pine Bluff and New Orleans Rail Road.—Length 160 miles. From Little Rock through Pine Bluff, to Eunice, on the Mississippi river; 20 miles of track laid, iron purchased for 40 miles more, and under the able management of its president, Col. J. M. Lewis, is being rapidly constructed to its terminus.

4. *Mississippi, Ouachita and Red River Rail Road.*—Length 170 miles; from Eunice on the Mississippi river to a point on Red River, near the western border of the State. Col. Jas. M. Lewis is also president of this road, which is a sufficient guarantee that it will be rapidly constructed, and the work done in a first class manner. Forty-two miles of this road is completed, and 20 miles more graded, bridged and ready for the iron. The completed portion of the road is now doing a large and prosperous business, transporting over 200 bales of cotton daily to Eunice. The business of the road will be very large and profitable, running, as it does, through a country second to none in fertility.

5. *Arkansas Central Rail Road.*—Length 150 miles; from Helena on the Mississippi river, thence to Aberdeen, on White river, and thence to Little Rock; and thence on, across the State, due west, to the western boundary; and through the Indian nation to the intersection of the Missouri, Kansas and Texas rail road near Boggy Depot; with a branch from Aberdeen, on White river, to Pine Bluff; distance, 50 miles. This road, under the management of Col. Dorsey, will be hurried to completion. Forty miles is completed, and the 110 miles more, to carry it west to Little Rock, is under contract to be finished this year.

The branch is also being rapidly pushed forward to Pine Bluff. The portion from Little Rock west, is not yet under contract; but its construction *may* be early looked for if Col. Dorsey continues in charge.

6. *Kansas City and Fort Smith Rail Road.*—From Fort Smith, on the western border of the State, due north to the State line; there connecting with the Missouri branch from Kansas City. This is an important road, running through the best developed grain and fruit counties in western Arkansas; and will be of immense advantage to Fort Smith. We are assured by the directors, that the road will be completed in eighteen months from date.

7. *Cairo and Fulton Railroad.*—From Cairo, Illinois, through southeast Missouri and northeast Arkansas, via. Poca-

hontas and Jacksonport, to Little Rock, and thence southwest across the State to Fulton, on Red river; from there to Jefferson and Marshall, Texas, and thence across the State of Texas to Lavedo, on the Rio Grande.

This is one of the grandest, and when completed, will be one of the best paying railroads in the United States, by reason of its location, the great richness of country through which it runs, and by its tapping and intersecting with every railroad in Arkansas and Texas. The entire length of the line will be about eight hundred and eighty miles. It will cross, in its course, the St. Louis and Belmont road, Iron Mountain and Helena road, intersect with the St. Louis, Iron Mountain and Little Rock road; crosses the Memphis and Kansas City and White River Valley and Texas railroads; at Little Rock, connecting with nine main trunk roads; at Fulton connecting with the Mississippi, Ouachita and Red River railroad; at Jefferson, Texas, with the Vicksburg, Shreveport and Texas road; at Marshall, with the Southern Pacific, and in its route from Marshall to Lavedo, will cross, intersect and connect with eight railroads in Texas.

The country along the line of this road is as rich as any country in the world in soil, minerals, timber. stone, etc. The cultivated portion along the line produces annually large crops of cotton, grain, tobacco, stock, fruit, etc. The uncultivated lands are covered by a magnificent growth of pine, black walnut, oak, ash, cherry, poplar and other useful timber. The whole country adjacent to the route abounds with coal, iron ore, fire clay and other valuable minerals. The whole length of this road, both in Missouri, Arkansas and Texas, runs through as fine a country as man can wish for, and nature could do but little more. The through business of this road will be immense, but it is to develop the richest portions of Arkansas, and open up a country whose way-business will tax to its utmost capacity a single track to accommodate. The country along its line will rapidly fill up with industrious farmers, enterprising miners and manufacturers, and the building of furnaces and factories, with thriving villages, towns and cities along its line, will afford an abundant traffic for a railroad. Northward bound trains will be ladened with cotton, sugar, tropical fruits, stock, lumber and minerals. The southward bound trains will be ladened with merchandise, grain, coal, etc. Every mile of this road, as it extends south from Little Rock, will pay from the start. Colonel Thomas Allen, the railroad king of Missouri, with his associates, are rapidly pushing it to completion. It is under contract to be finished to Little Rock by July 1st, 1872, and to Fulton by January 1st, 1874. With a land grant three hundred and one miles long by forty miles wide, the early completion of this road is an assured fact.

8. *St. Louis and Little Rock Railroad.*—From Cuba City, on the Atlantic and Pacific railroad, running south through Missouri, entering Arkansas in Fulton county, thence through Batesville to Little Rock. It will run through counties remarkably rich in agriculture and mineral wealth, and will be of great advantage, not only to the counties through which it will run, but to Little Rock, bringing a large trade to this city that has heretofore went to Memphis.

9. *Iron Mountain and Helena Railroad.*—From St. Louis, via. Iron Mountain railroad, through Missouri, and entering Arkansas in Green county; thence through Craighead, Poinsett, St. Francis and Phillips counties to Helena. This road has a bright future, a munificent land subscription, embracing thousands of acres of some of the best lands in that portion of the State, besides a large local monied subscription, made by the counties through which it runs. This road will be of immense advantage to that portion of the State, opening up for settlement a country equal to the celebrated blue grass region of Kentucky, not only for grass but for grains, fruits and cotton.

10. *St. Louis, Iron Mountain and Little Rock Railroad.*—From St. Louis, via. the Iron Mountain railroad, through Arkansas to Little Rock. This is another of Colonel Thomas Allen's roads, and that is a sufficient guarantee that it will be pushed forward to completion.

11. Memphis and Kansas City Railroad.—From Memphis, Tenn., through Jacksonport, Batesville, Yellville and into Missouri to Springfield, and thence to Kansas City. This road is under contract, and forty or more miles ready for the iron. It runs through a fine country, the celebrated White river valley, and is in the hands of energetic and monied men, who will hurry it through to completion.

12. Memphis, Shreveport and Texas Railroad.—From Memphis, through DeVall's Bluff, Pine Bluff, Camden and Shreveport, and on into Texas.

13. Little Rock and Hot Springs Railroad.—From Little Rock to Hot Springs, distance sixty miles. This road will be of great importance to both places and the intermediate country, rendering travel to that celebrated watering place easy and rapid, and opening up a rich mineral country. The immense travel to Hot Springs demands the immediate construction of this road.

14. Little Rock and Shreveport Railroad.—From Little Rock, via. Camden, to Shreveport, running through a fine agricultural and mineral country, and at Shreveport connecting with the Louisiana and Texas railroad. The lawful amount of the capital stock has been subscribed, and the company are now ready to go to work.

15. White River Valley and Texas Railroad.—From Batesville, on White river, via. DeVall's Bluff, to Pine Bluff, and thence direct to Texas, via. Shreveport and Marshall, running through a country second to none in fertility and productiveness.

16. Arkansas and Louisiana Rail Road.—From Little Rock, due south, through Arkansas, to Alexandria, Louisiana; thence to Opelousas, Berwick's Bay, to New Orleans; connecting the warm Gulf, via Little Rock, with the frozen regions of the north.

17. Illinois, Missouri and Texas Rail Road.—From Cape Girardeau, on the Mississippi river, through south-east Missouri and north Arkansas, to Van Buren, near the western boundary of the State.

Here are seventeen rail roads, one completed, and all the others in a fair way soon to be. From the amount of work performed the last year, and the present prospects, it is safe to say, that the completion of all these rail roads in a short time will be an accomplished fact. Several other companies have charters for rail roads, that will also be built.

The above described, are all main trunk rail roads, and are not second in importance to any rail roads in the south-west. When these are completed, every portion of the State will be accommodated with rail road facilities, and will open to settlement the finest portions of the State; rich in agricultural, and peculiarly rich in mineral wealth; and will add millions to the wealth of Arkansas, binding its people together in bonds of mutual interest; thus rendering them a happy, wealthy, and prosperous people. And we hesitate not to say, that in less than five years these rail roads will all be built. But assuming that, for cause, some of them will be longer in completion, what State affords so great and varied inducements as this? To live in Arkansas will no longer be out of the world, or behind the times, in the possession of information in regard to great events. The whistle of a rail road locomotive will awaken new life in a region of country hitherto of little importance in the busy world.

A look at the map will show the reader what a vast area of rich, "ever bearing" soil is commanded by these rail roads and their connections—connecting, on the south and west, with the rich soils of Louisiana, Texas and the Indian Nation. In every direction, and in every portion of the State, men are quietly engaged in extending the rail road system of the State; expanding and developing regions of country, which will soon furnish homes to thousands of people; and increasing, to an incalculable extent, the wealth and resources of the State. All of which will have a direct tendency in building up Little Rock, the chief commercial center, and other well located towns of the State.

Arkansas has now on foot and well under way, a system of rail roads through the length and width of its domain that, when completed, will not fall far below 4000 miles, and their progress at this time is greater than at any former period. We have always contended that the thirty-fifth parallel route would be the best at all seasons of the year, for the successful operation of a Pacific rail road. And to-day, the Atlantic and Pacific rail road is constructing their line on that route, almost due west from Little Rock. The Memphis and Little Rock, and Little Rock and Fort Smith rail roads, connecting at Fort Smith with a road to the Atlantic and Pacific rail road, near the Canadian river, places central Arkansas in direct connection, and on the main through line to the Pacific. To sum up, this will be truly the shortest and best route between the Atlantic and Pacific; and over this route, through Arkansas, will come the heavily ladened trains of valuable goods from the East Indies.

What an influence the construction and operation of all these rail roads will have upon the now partially unknown regions through which they will pass. Can this not be foreseen by the people of Arkansas, who know most of the country? It can, but we will leave our readers to imagine for themselves, the great changes that will then be inaugurated in this rich and beautiful country; and what chances there are now for immigrants from other States and Europe to come in and possess themselves of land, rich in all the elements of agriculture, and which will, before ten years, increase in value more than ten fold. Were the resources, health and general advantages of our State more fully known, the tide of immigration would turn from the west to the south-west, and our hundreds of thousands of acres of as fertile soil as the sun shines on, now vacant, would provide happy homes for multitudes of the sons and daughters of Europe and America.

The building of rail roads in Arkansas is an event which opens to us a new and bright future, Henceforward, by reason of an easy and rapid communication with all parts of the country, this State, with its mild and salubrious climate; with its fine, pure water and numerous streams; with its rich mineral wealth; with its fine fruit of every description; and with its rich and fertile soil, invites the enterprising and energetic man to make it his home, and unite with us in advancing its material prosperity.

The bright and happy future, the subject of our wishes for many long years, is just beginning to dawn upon us! No longer then, shall we be compelled to give one-half of our surplus crops to transport the other half to market. No longer shall we be compelled to travel by stage to reach the outside world. No longer shall we then be compelled to pay heavy prices for the transportation of such merchandise as we shall need. To the capital, skill, energy and perseverence of the directors of our rail roads, we shall be indebted for the great benefits we are now about to enjoy; and to enjoy the great benefits, we cordially invite the immigrant from every State. No portion of the Union surpasses this State in natural advantages.

Arkansas has a deep interest in the success of her rail road system. It will bring people and money, energy and progress to the State; and this is the principal want of this region to become a delightful land. The way trade of these roads, to say nothing of the through business which will flow through the State from their connections, would alone enrich the State. Our rail road system, when perfected, will present the shortest and best connected route between Chicago and St. Louis, and New Orleans, and other gulf ports; and the States of Texas, California and intervening Territories, will be brought nearer to New York, Boston and the east, than by any other route that can be built.

The benefits of railroads, all admit. Hence the anxiety of aspiring communities to bring the inspiring voice of the locomotive to their doors. The railroad renders possible the colonization and settlement of countries the most remote. It reclaims deserts; it peoples territories; it builds up States. Along its line cities are buoyant with the full feeling of vigorous growth and prosperity. Commercial marts are filled with opulence and trade. Railroads help the country as well as the towns, and are the settler's best friend. They enrich the farmer as well as the merchant, and add immeasurably to personal comfort and independence, and the aggregate wealth of the community and the State. They impoverish none and enrich all. They add a hundred fold to the value of the farmer's real estate, and afford him rapid and easy transportation for his surplus produce to remunerative markets. They lift him from dependence and servitude to opulence and independence. Without railroads how could Kansas have been settled, or Iowa made wealthy and prosperous? What would central Illinois be to-day without railroads? a vast ocean waste of prairie, a dead sea of inactivity. What benefits Kansas, Iowa or Illinois, have derived from their railroads, Arkansas will soon derive from her's, only, at least ten fold more so. Does Kansas or Iowa have one mile of navigable water course within their domain? No. Do they have immense forests of the finest timber in the Union for manufacturing purposes? No. Do they have rich and extensive mines of iron, lead, copper, zinc, manganese, marble, kaolin, marl, slate, rock-crystals and coal? No. Do they have so much splendid water power, do they have richer or more fruitful soil? No. Do they have as favorable climate? No. Can they raise so great a variety of the fruits of the earth? No. Can they compete with Arkansas in stock raising, fruit growing or manufacturing? No. Can the emigrant acquire a home easier or cheaper in Kansas or Iowa, than in Arkansas? No. Then, don't Arkansas offer superior inducements to those States for capitalists, skilled laborers and farmers, to come to this State and secure a home and wealth? Those north-western States have just this advantage, they are principally prairie, and offer to the settler a farm ready for the plow, but farmers cannot get along very well without timber for houses, barns, fences, and for fuel, neither can they get rich growing corn, wheat, oats, etc., away some distance from thriving towns for a market; and what is to sustain a thriving town, but timber, minerals and coal, for manufacturing? Their growth and progress are mainly dependent upon railways. So is Arkansas, to a certain extent, but at the same time affording to railroads a remunerative and productive business from the beginning. The advantages of the railroad system of Arkansas, when completed, can hardly be over-estimated. Coursing, as they do, rich and productive lands, underlaid with a great variety of valuable minerals; shaded by forests of the finest timber known to mechanical uses, they cannot fail to fill this beautiful State with thriving towns and thrifty farm settlements. The magnificent lands of this State must soon be occupied and settled upon by industrious people, who will cause them to teem and blossom with fertility and productiveness. Towns and cities will spring up like magic, and grow and expand into great centers of trade and manufacture. The interest of the railroads and the people of a State are mutual. What enriches one benefits the other.

DESCRIPTION OF COUNTIES

ARKANSAS COUNTY.

This county is bounded on the north-east by White river, and the Arkansas runs through the southern portion; the greater portion of this county is prairie, with slight ridge-like elevations, and river bottoms; the soil yields 1800 pounds of seed cotton, or 40 to 50 bushels of corn to the acre; by a good system of drainage the soil may be made highly productive. Timber—gum, hackberry, box-elder, etc. The first settlement in Arkansas was made at Arkansas Post, in this county; population of the county, in 1870, 8,268. De Witt is the county site.

ASHLEY.

This county adjoins the State of Louisiana on the south, land generally level; timber, pine, oak, gum, etc.; soil fine for cotton and corn; population 8,042. Hamburg is the county site; coal, copper and lead, have been discovered and worked in this county.

BENTON.

This is the extreme north-western county. Bentonville is the county site; population 13,831; character of the county is that of a plateau, divided into a series of ridges, by numerous clear creeks; soil favorable for agriculture; corn produces 40 to

60 bushels, and wheat 15 to 20 bushels to the acre; and 1,000 to 1,500 pounds of tobacco to the acre; also, fine crops of oats and hay; good for fruits of all kinds; timber, over-cup oak, black, red and white oak, ash, linden, etc.; under growth, hazel, shumate and grape vines. Fort Smith and Kansas City railroad will run through this county from south to north.

BOONE

Is situated east of Marion county and adjoining Missouri; population 7,032. Harrison is the county site. Land, a plateau, soil rich and productive, yielding fine crops of cotton, corn, wheat, oats and hay; splendid for fruit and stock raising; Memphis and Kansas City railroad will run through the county. Rich in minerals.

BRADLEY

Lies in the southern portion; population 8,646. Warren is the county site; timber, post and black oak, pine, elm, hickory and ash; undergrowth, dogwood, muscadine and other grape vines, in great abundance; soil produces 1,500 pounds of seed cotton, 40 bushels corn, or 15 bushels of wheat to the acre; lignite coal beds, 6 feet thick, gypsum, gypseous marl and tertiary shell marl, are found in this county. The Arkansas and Louisiana railroad will run through the edge of the county, and the Mississippi, Ouachita and Red river railroad is nearly finished from Eunice to Warren.

CALHOUN

Adjoins Bradley on the east. Population 3,853. Hampton is the county site; timber, white, red, post and black oak, and pine; soil produces 1,000 pounds of seed cotton, or 40 bushels of corn to the acre. Arkansas and Louisiana railroad will run through a portion of the county.

CARROLL

Adjoins Missouri on the north. Population 5,780. Carrollton

is the county site; timber, over-cup, black and scarlet oak, elm, mockernut and black gum, with pawpaw, elder and grape vines in abundance; land rolling and hilly, prairie and timber; soil rich, produces 50 to 60 bushels of corn, 15 to 25 bushels of wheat and 35 bushels of oats or rye to the acre; excellent for hay, fine for fruit; splendid for stock, especially for sheep; a great number could be raised here. The Memphis and Kansas City railroad will run through or near this county. Rich mines of iron, lead and marble exist here.

CHICOT

Lies in the extreme southeast, and bounded by the Mississippi on the east; population, 7,214. Columbia is the county site. Timber, gum and button-wood; land generally level, soil "buckshot land" and rich alluvial river bottoms, finest cotton land in this part of the State, that article being the principal crop, producing from one and a half to two bales to the acre; and as a consequence, the reclaimed lands are rapidly advancing in price. The Little Rock, Pine Bluff and New Orleans railroad and the Mississippi, Ouachita and Red River railroad run through the county.

CLARK

Lies in the south center of the State; population, 11,953. Arkadelphia is the county site. Timber, gum, hickory, pin and Spanish oak, ash and sea ash. Land hilly, broken and level; soil very productive, producing fifty bushels of corn, twenty bushels of wheat, or one bale of cotton to the acre; rich in minerals; limestone in abundance, and great quantities of lime burned. The Cairo and Fulton railroad will run through the center of the county, and when completed, will render this county very attractive.

COLUMBIA

Lies in the extreme southern portion of the State; population, 11,397. Magnolia is the county site. Timber, holly, beech, pine and oak; land level, with some ridges; soil rich, producing fine crops of cotton. The Shreveport, Little Rock and Memphis railroad will run through this county.

CONWAY.

This county lies on the north side of the Arkansas river, adjoining Pulaski county on the west; population, 8,112. Springfield is the county site, and Lewisburg its largest town and chief shipping point. Timber, hickory, white, black and post oak, land hilly, and bottom soil rich, producing fine crops of cotton, corn, wheat and oats, also fine for fruit and stock. Coal and other minerals are found here. This is a choice county, and deserves the attention of immigrants. The Little Rock and Fort Smith railroad now runs daily trains through the county.

CRAWFORD

Lies on the north side of the Arkansas river, and extends to the western boundary of the State. Population, 8,957. Van Buren is its chief town and county site, and does a large trade with the country north to near the Missouri line; its merchants are substantial business men. Timber, yellow pine, Spanish, white, black, red and post oak, hickory, walnut and black gum; land in the northern part hilly, in the southern, bottoms and ridges; soil rich, producing large crops of cotton, corn, wheat, oats and hay, also producing fine crops of fruit. Four railroads will run through the county. This county is rich in iron, lead, coal and other minerals; its rich soil and rich underground wealth, with its healthfulness, will make this a rich and populous county.

CRITTENDEN.

This county lies on the Mississippi, opposite Memphis, Tenn.; population, 3,831. Marion is the county site. Timber, large oak, hickory, sassafras, hackberry and *cane*. The celebrated Crowley's ridge passes through this county, but level land predominates. Many small lakes and bayous are interspersed through the interior, requiring drainage. The soil is very rich, and produces large crops of cotton, corn, wheat and hay. The Memphis and Little Rock railroad runs through, and the Iron Mountain and Memphis railroad is building through this county.

CRAIGHEAD

Lies in the northeast part of the State; population 4,577. Jonesboro is the county site. Timber, walnut, ash, hickory, gum, white, black and post oak, poplar, etc. Crowley's ridge passes through this county from north to south. The land lies in broad upland plateaus, with numerous clear, cold springs; soil, rich alluvial and highly productive, producing cotton, corn, wheat, oats and the grasses, fruits, etc.; also a fine stock county. The Iron Mountain and Helena railroad will run through the center of this county.

DALLAS

Lies in the south center of the State. Princeton is the county site; population, 5,707. Timber, hickory, oak, ash, walnut, gum and elm. Land, some portions hilly, but ridges and bottoms predominate; soil rich, producing fine crops of cotton, corn, wheat and oats; rich in minerals. The Shreveport and Memphis railroad will run through this county. The salt wells of this county have been worked successfully.

DESHA

Lies on the Mississippi, at the mouth of the Arkansas; population, 6,125. Napoleon is the county site. Timber, gum, buttonwood, etc.; land level, but admits of easy drainage; soil rich alluvial cotton land, and produces that staple in abundance, yielding one and a half to two bales to the acre: has good water transportation. The Little Rock, Pine Bluff and New Orleans railroad runs through this county.

DREW

Adjoins Desha on the west; population 9,960. Monticello is the county site. Timber, hickory, gum, pine, red and black oak; land nearly level, prairie and timber; soil, gravelly loam, gum land, considered best for cotton, producing one bale to the acre, or forty to fifty bushels of corn. The Little Rock, Pine Bluff and New Orleans railroad runs through the northern part of this county.

FRANKLIN

Lies in the northwest, on both sides of the Arkansas river; population, 9,627. Ozark is the county site. Timber, walnut sweet gum, maple, white and black oak; land somewhat broken, but there are fine bottoms of rich soil; products, cotton, corn, wheat, oats and hay. This is one of the rich coal counties, being found in great abundance within one mile of Ozark, three feet thick of clear coal; also iron and other minerals. The Little Rock and Fort Smith railroad runs through this county, and over the coal lands, which will make them valuable by reason of the facilities for transportation afforded.

FULTON

Adjoins Missouri on the north; population, 4,843. Pilot Hill is the county site. Timber, red, black and white oak, hickory, ash, grape vines and hazel; land, a series of ridges and valleys, with clear running streams; soil, mulatto-barren, soft permeable, producing abundant crops of corn, fifty to sixty bushels, and wheat twenty-five to thirty bushels to the acre; splendid for fruit; good for stock, especially sheep; rich in minerals and metals. The celebrated Mammoth Spring is here. The St. Louis, Batesville and Little Rock railroad will run through the eastern part of this county.

GREEN

Lies in the extreme north-east; population 7,513. Gainsville is the county site. Timber, white, red, black and post oak;

poplar, walnut, ash, hazel and grape vines. The land is rolling; soil very rich, producing fine crops of cotton, corn, wheat, oats, grapes and fruits. Fine county for stock. The Iron Mountain and Helena rail road runs through the county.

HEMPSTEAD

Lies in the south-west; population 13,768. Washington is the county site, and also the land office for the Washington district, is located here. Timber, pine, gum, walnut, beech and Spanish oak. Land rolling; ridges and bottoms are fine cotton lands. Here is the celebrated Red river cotton or hog wallow land, producing from one to one and a half bales to the acre; and 50 to 60 bushels of corn. The Cairo and Fulton rail road will run through the center of the county.

HOT SPRING

Is south of center from Little Rock; population 5,877. Rockport is the county site. Timber, oak, hickory and dogwood. The land is mountainous; this county is one of the intensely mineral counties of the State. The celebrated Hot Springs, 54 in number are situated in this county. There is probably no portion of Arkansas that affords a greater variety of minerals than Magnet cove, in this county. Here are found novaculite rock or hone stone, titanic acid, black garnets, quartz, agate, iron pyrites, magnetic iron ore, slate, limestone, etc; here is an immense bed of magnetic iron ore, some of which exhibits polarity, believed to be as extensive as Iron mountain, in Missouri. This is a remarkable county in its great variety and extent of minerals. The Cairo and Fulton rail road, and Hot Springs and Little Rock rail road will run through this county. The Salt Springs have been worked successfully for years past.

INDEPENDENCE

Is situated in the north-east part of the State, on both sides of White river; population 14,566. Batesville is the county site.

The United States land office is also located here. Timber, walnut, elm, hackberry, scaly bark hickory, and box elder. Land is hilly, with valleys and broad river bottoms; the soil most valuable and fertile, producing large crops of cotton, corn, wheat and oats; grass, of all kinds, yields large crops. The soil must be classed among the richest in the State, splendid for fruit and stock. Lead and other metal deposits exist here in rich beds. The Memphis and Kansas city, and St. Louis and Little Rock rail roads, will run through this county. These, with White river, afford ample facilities for trade and commerce. Batesville will become an important city.

IZARD

Adjoins Independence on the north-west; population 6,806. Mt. Olive is the county site. Timber, walnut, elm, red, black and white oak, hickory, ash, hazel and grape vines. Land, mountains, hills, valleys, and White river bottoms. Soil is rich, produces cotton, corn, wheat, rye, oats, and the grapes; fruits grow well. This county is good for sheep or any kind of stock; is also rich in minerals, especially lead. The Memphis and Kansas City rail road will run through the county. White river runs through the center, and with the rail road, will furnish facilities for trade and commerce.

JACKSON

Lies on White river; population 7,268. Jacksonport is the county site. Timber, elm, ash, hickory, walnut, red and black oak. The land is mostly level, with some hills in the north. The soil is very rich; some farms having been cultivated for 60 years, and still produce large crops of cotton. The products are cotton, corn, oats, hay and fruits. The Cairo and Fulton rail road will run through the county.

JEFFERSON

Lies on both sides of the Arkansas river; population 15,733.

Pine Bluff is the county site. The land is mostly level, and the soil is extraordinarily rich in the elements of vegetable food; black elm, ash, oak and hickory land, furnishing the finest cotton land in the south, producing from one to two bales of cotton to the acre; corn, 50 to 60 bushels; also, good crops of oats and hay. The Little Rock, Pine Bluff and New Orleans, Memphis and Shreveport, and branch of the Arkansas Central from Aberdeen, will all run through the county. Pine Bluff is a large and flourishing city, and surrounded, as it is, by a fine country, will be a considerable city.

JOHNSON

Lies on the north side of the Arkansas river, in the western portion of the State; population 9,152. Clarksville is the county site. Timber, sweet gum, cherry, walnut, laurel, oak, hickory, pine, post, and white oak, hazel and cane. Land is mountains, ridges, and bottoms very fertile, producing one bale of cotton, thirty to fifty bushels of corn, twenty bushels of wheat, forty of oats to the acre. The prairies furnish natural meadows for stock and hay, rich in iron, coal, and other minerals. The celebrated Spadra coal and iron mines are in this county, close to the Arkansas river. Little Rock and Fort Smith Railroad is building through this county.

LAFAYETTE

Is the extreme south-west county; population 9,130. Lewisville is the county site. Timber, gum, walnut, cane and grape vines. The land is prairie and timber, almost level. Soil is remarkably rich, but needs draining. This county embraces considerable of the celebrated red cotton land of Red river bottoms, producing large crops of cotton; good for corn and hay. The Cairo and Fulton rail road will run through the county.

LAWRENCE

Lies in the north-east; population 5,981. Smithville is the

county site. Timber, poplar, walnut, red, black, white and post oak. The land is a plateau, divided by ridges into valleys, with clear streams. The soil of the valleys is very rich ; the uplands are also good, especially for the grains and fruits ; and fine for stock. Products, cotton, corn, wheat, oats, rye, barley and grapes. This county is rich in minerals—iron, copper and lead. The Hoppe zinc and copper mines are in this county. The Cairo and Fulton rail road runs through the eastern part of the county, giving rail road facilities to the county over a first class road.

MADISON

Lies in the north-west ; population 7,937. Huntsville is the county site. Timber, black jack, post oak and hickory, with hazel and grape vines. The land is divided between mountains, hills and fertile valleys. The soil is well adapted for the cereals, fruits and stock raising, especially sheep. Rich in minerals of iron, lead, copper, zinc and coal. The Fayetteville district land office is located at Huntsville.

MARION

Adjoins Missouri on the north ; population 3,979. Yellville is the county site. Timber, post, black, and white oak, hickory, hazel, pawpaw and grape vines. The land is broken into hills, ridges and valleys. The soil is good for all kinds of grains and grasses ; and on White river bottoms for cotton. This is also a good county for fruits, especially the grape. A fine county for stock, as the soil is clothed with a luxuriant vegetation of rich grass. The Memphis and Kansas City rail road will run through this county.

MISSISSPPI

Lies in the north-east panhandle of the State and bounded by the Mississippi river on the east, and the State of Missouri on the north; population 3,633. Oceola is the county site; timber, large oak, hickory, hackberry and cane; land for the most part composed of alluvial soils, subject to inundation at high freshets of the Mississippi; there are many small lakes and bayous in the interior, where the soil is known as buck-shot land; produces cotton, corn and hay, yielding large crops. St. Louis, Iron Mountain and Memphis railroad will run through the county.

MONROE

Lies on both sides of White river, north of Arkansas county; population 8,336. Aberdeen is the county site, and will be an important city; located on White river, and connected east and west by the Arkansas Central railroad, also, the junction of the Pine Bluff branch of the Arkansas Central railroad, gives it great facilities for transportation; timber, button-wood, ash, overcup oak, mulberry, cane and pawpaw; soil rich; bottoms and table land; products, cotton, corn and hay; good for oats. Two railroads and White river run through the county.

MONTGOMERY

Is situated in the south-west; population 2,988. Mt. Ida, is the county site; timber, hickory, white and post oak and dogwood; This is a mountainous county, rich in mineral, of iron, lead, etc.; the celebrated rock crystals come from this county and are found in great abundance. There are fine quarries of marble; four or five mineral springs exist here. The most fertile portion of the county is Caddo Cove, where fine crops are raised.

NEWTON

Is situated in the north-west; population 3,364. Jasper is the county site; timber, hickory, ash and grape vines; land rolling, hilly, rocky and small valleys; soil good for grain and fruits; fine for stock, as there are numerous clear streams; products, corn, wheat, oats, rye; rich mines of lead ore are worked here; county rich in minerals. Cape Girardeau, Van Buren and Texas railroad will run through the county.

OUACHITA

Is situated in the south.west; population 12,975. Camden is the county site; Washita river runs through the county and affords steamboat navigation to Arkadelphia, two-thirds of the year; timber, large pine, oak, beech, hickory, ash, dogwood, cane and yellow basswood; land rolling and fine bottoms; soil rich, producing one to one and a half bales of cotton, or 50 to 60 bushels of corn to the acre; good for hay; lignite coal beds, 6 feet thick, and of a good quality, exist here, and have been mined extensively in times past. Little Rock, Shreveport and Memphis railroad will run through the county, crossing Washita river at Camden.

PERRY

Lies on the south bank of the Arkansas river, north-west of Pulaski county; population 2,684. Perryville is the county site; land mountainous and hilly; timber, pine, hickory and post-oak, with grape vines; soil produces one bale of cotton, 40 bushels of corn or 30 bushels of oats to the acre; well adapted for fruit, especially grapes. This county being so near Little Rock, will have rare facilities for disposing of her surplus products at good prices at Little Rock. This county is located in the coal basin of Arkansas.

PHILLIPS

Lies in the east center of the State, on the Mississippi river. Helena is the county site; population 15,372. The land office for the Helena district is located at Helena, in this county. Crowley's ridge terminates below Helena, and from its base flow numerous clear, cold springs. "In an agricultural point of view, this county ranks equal to any in the State. The alluvial bottom soil produces one bale of cotton, or 50 to 75 bushels of corn to the acre; on Crowley's ridge, 40 to 45 bushels of corn, and 20 to 30 bushels of wheat to the acre, and is excellent for rye and oats. Timber, large poplar, beech, oaks, walnut, gum, sugar tree, honey lucust and cane." Helena is now, and will become an important city; situated on the Mississippi river, and having rail connections with Mobile, St. Louis, Little Rock and the south, will build her up to be a large commercial city. Two rail roads run through the county.

PIKE

Situated in the south-west; population 3,788. Murfreesboro is the county site. The land in the northern part is hilly, in the southern portion, table land and fine creek bottoms. Timber, principally oak and hickory. The soil is good, producing fine crops of cotton, corn, wheat and oats. This is a rich mineral county, consisting of iron, lead, limestone, gypseous marl, slate and valuable beds of gypsum. Little river affords splendid water power, and years ago, a cotton factory was built on that stream in this county. The Cairo and Fulton rail road will run through the southern portion of this county.

POINSETT

Lies in the north-east; population 1,720. Boliver is the county site. The land is rolling; Crowly's ridge runs through the county from north to south. The soil is rich and well adapted to the cereals, grasses and fruits. Timber, poplar, walnut, oak and maple. The St. Louis, Iron Mountain and Helena rail road will run through the county.

POLK

Is situated in the west center, adjoining the Indian nation. Dallas is the county site; population 3,306. The land is rugged and mountainous, and rich in minerals of iron, lead, limestone and hone stone. The timber consists of walnut, cherry, pine, oak, elm and hickory. The products are cotton, corn and sweet potatoes.

POPE.

West of Conway county, on the north side of the river, lies

Pope; population, 8,409. Dover is the county site. Norristown, Galla Rock and Georgetown are the chief business towns. Land, hilly and broad river bottoms; soil of the bottoms very rich, producing one to one and a half bales of cotton, or fifty to sixty bushels of corn to the acre; upland fine for wheat, grass and fruits; timber, oak, hickory, walnut, ash and dogwood. The Little Rock and Fort Smith railroad is now building through the county. Rich coal fields are situated here. Large quanties of cotton are exported from this county.

PRAIRIE

Lies near the center of the State, east of and adjoining Pulaski county; population, 5,604. Brownsville is the county site. Land, rolling prairie and timber; growth, oak, ash, hickory and dogwood; soil productive, yielding large crops of cotton, corn, wheat, oats and hay, and well adapted for fruits. The Memphis and Little Rock railroad runs through the center of the county; also, the Arkansas Central will run through the southern portion of the county. The situation of this county, so near the city of Little Rock, renders it very attractive to immigrants, affording a good market for all the products of the soil.

PULASKI

Is the central county of the State, situated on both sides of the river; population in 1860, 11,699; in 1870, 32,066, and now containing not less than 40,000 inhabitants, and increasing in population at a wonderful rate. Land that can now be bought at five dollars per acre will, in a few years, sell for fifty, yes, one hundred dollars per acre. This county offers advantages not equaled by any county in the State, or in the whole south or west, for the farmer, laborer, mechanic or capitalist. With the Arkansas river running through the center, from northwest to southeast, and twelve trunk railroads built, building and projected to Little Rock, running through every portion of the county, giving facilities for shipping to a good market; and the completion of these roads will add immensely to the value of every foot of land in the entire county. Little Rock is the county site. The land, for the greater portion, is a broad plateau, rising in easy undulations from the river bottoms. The bottoms are exceedingly fertile, producing one to one and a half bales of cotton, or fifty to seventy-five bushels of corn to the acre; timber of the bottoms, black walnut, red oak, sweet gum, red mulberry and linden; undergrowth, pawpaw, elder bushes and grape vines; upland growth, pin, post, white and black oak, hickory, sassafras and grape vines, and the soil produces twenty-five bushels of wheat, or thirty-five bushels of corn to the acre; good for oats, and well adapted for fruits. The variety and richness of the minerals of this county are not excelled by any county in the southwest. The limonite iron ore assays 51.70 per cent. of iron; pisolite ore assays 47.39 of iron. There are fine bodies of iron ore in all parts of the county. The celebrated Kellogg lead and silver mines are also located here. There are immense deposits of white kaolin, or porcelain clay, quarries of roofing slate, and the best of building granite, and limestone, for burning lime, fire clay for brick, and every mineral and metal useful in the arts or necessary for building up and sustaining the commerce of a large city, as Little Rock will certainly become, located in the county within easy access of the city.

RANDOLPH

Is located in the northeast, adjoining Missouri; population, 7,466. Pocahontas is the county site. Timber, black walnut, large white and black oaks, white and black gum; land rolling, with low ridges and valleys; soil rich, producing large crops of cotton, corn, wheat, oats, rye and hay; fruits grow well and produce fine crops. Black river runs through the center of the county, and is navigable for steamboats during the greater portion of the year to Pocahontas. The Cairo and Fulton railroad and the Iron Mountain and Little Rock railroad run through this county.

ST. FRANCIS

Is situated in the eastern portion of the State; population, 6,414. Madison, is the county site, located on the Memphis and Little Rock railroad, and also at the crossing of the Iron Mountain and Helena railroad. Land, in the eastern portion, broken and hilly; the balance of the county is clay ridges and bottoms; soil rich, especially the ridges; so are the bottoms, but need draining, and produce one bale of cotton, forty to fifty bushels of corn, or fifteen bushels of wheat to the acre, and is also good for oats, red top and timothy; timber, hickory, gum, poplar, ash, elm, sassafras, dogwood and box elder. In minerals, there are beds of iron ore, and valuable beds of shell marl.

SALINE

Lies southwest of Pulaski county; population, 3,911. Benton is the county site. Land cut up into hills, ridges and valleys; timber, oak, hickory and pine; the soil produces forty bushels of corn, fifteen to twenty bushels of wheat to the acre, and good for oats. This is, also, an intensely mineral county; immense quarries of marble, slate and granite exist here, also limonite iron ore, lead and lignite beds. The situation of this county, between Little Rock and Hot Springs, and the two or three railroads projected through it, will greatly enhance the value of property and render it attractive to the immigrant.

SCOTT

Lies in the western portion of the State; population 7,483. Waldron is the county site. Land rolling, some portions broken, others valleys and bottoms; soil vèry productive, producing cotton, corn and wheat, good for oats and fruits; timber, oak, hickory, pine and ash. The Arkansas Central railroad will run through the county.

SEARCY

Is situated in the north by west; population, 6,614. Lebanon is the county site. Land, a plateau, with some hills; soil fine for the grains, grasses and fruits; well adapted to stock raising, especially sheep, as vegetation remains green most all the year. Here is the home of the grape, and all the fruits. The minerals are abundant here, such as iron, lead, coal, marble, etc. The Illinois, Missouri and Texas railroad will run through the county.

SEVIER

Lies in the southwest, adjoining the Indian Nation; population, 4,492. Paraclifta is the county site. Land mountainous and hilly, with narrow valleys in the northern part; the southern is gently rolling or mostly level. The black lands in this county are exceedingly fertile, producing one bale of cotton, fifty to sixty bushels of corn to the acre; one field of 250 acres yielded 325 bales of cotton; the upland soil produces thirty-five bushels of corn or twenty bushels of wheat to the arce. This county is remarkably rich in minerals. Here are the Bellah lead and silver mines; the ore assays 73 per cent. of lead. A ton of lead yielded 52½ ounces of silver. A ton of this ore, sent to England, yielded 73 per cent of lead and 148 ounces of silver. Slate quarries, superior to the best Vermont slate, chalk marl and marly limestone, beds of iron ore, and the Graham salt mines are also here. All these mines can be worked at a great profit. The Cairo and Fulton railroad will run near this county, and the Mississippi, Ouachita and Red River railroad will run through the county.

SHARP,

Formerly a part of Lawrence, lies west of that county; population, 5,400. Canton is the county site. Land, a plateau, divided into hills and valleys; soil excellent for the grains and grasses, and well adapted for fruit culture and stock raising. This county is rich in minerals; here is the American Zinc Company, of New York, with $1,000,000 capital, working with profit the mines located on a 2,000 acre tract, with splendid machinery and mills, and good houses, and several tons of zinc and copper ready for shipment. They have lead mines, now in operation, a smelter, and, in fact, everything necessary, and in good order, making as good lead as can be made anywhere. The sulphuret of zinc contains 63 per cent. of metal. The surrounding country has a nucleus in this operation for a home market for their productions, selling beef to the miners at five cents per pound, eggs at ten cents per dozen, and every thing else at an equally cheap rate. The St. Louis, Batesville and Little Rock railroad will run through the county.

UNION

Lies in the south, adjoining Louisiana; population, 10,571. El Dorado is the county site. Land, somewhat broken in the center, but the rest is nearly level; the soil produces one bale of cotton, 30 bushels of corn, or ten to fifteen bushels wheat to the acre; timber, beech, oak, gum, holly, pine and hazel. Iron ore, lignite and mineral springs are among the minerals of the county. Ouachita river affords facilities for shipping to market. The Arkansas and Louisiana railroad will run through the county. At Champagnolle, in this county, is located the land office for Ouachita district.

VAN BUREN

Lies in the north center of the State; population, 5,107. Clinton is the county site. Land rolling; soil produces fine crops of cotton, corn, wheat, oats and the grasses; splendid for fruit; timber, oak, ash, walnut, hickory and hazel; rich in minerals of iron, lead, marble and limestone.

WASHINGTON

Is situated in the northwest, adjoining the Indian Nation; population, 17,266. Fayetteville is the county site; a beautiful city, located on a hill overlooking the surrounding country for miles. The city contains 2,000 inhabitants, and is the location selected by the board of trustees for the Arkansas Industrial University, an institution that will be of great advantage to the city and county. The city is healthfully located; its business houses are principally constructed of brick, and the occupants do a large and profitable business. The people of this county, heretofore, have given more attention to mixed agriculture than perhaps any other county in the State; and its rapid increase in wealth and population show the most gratifying results; it also shows what can be done in other counties of the State. The land is broken into hills, ridges and valleys; soil exceedingly fertile; the products are corn, wheat, oats, barley, potatoes and fruit. The flour of this county is not excelled in the United States; and its Shannon and Kentucky Red apples are not equalled in the world. Here is a people that have become wealthy by diversifying their employments, and yet have only just commenced to develop the resources of the county. Timber, white, black, red and Spanish oak, pine, mockernut, chestnut, chincapin, persimmon, shellbark hickory and grape vines; minerals, iron, lead and coal. The Fort Smith and Kansas City railroad will run through the center of the county.

WHITE

Adjoins Pulaski on the northeast; population, 10,340. Searcy is the county site. Land rolling, with bottoms on the streams; soil rich and productive, yielding large crops of cotton, corn, wheat, oats and hay; good for fruit culture, and fine for stock; timber, oak, hickory, gum, ash and hazel and grape vines in abundance. The St. Louis and Little Rock railroad is completed through the county and cars running. Being situated near Little Rock, this county will rapidly increase in wealth and population.

WOODRUFF

Lies east of White and adjoining; populatiou, 6,891. Cotton Plant is the county site. Land rolling; soil rich, producing large crops of cotton, corn, oats and hay; good soil for fruits; will become a wealthy county, from its nearness to Little Rock. The Cairo and Fulton railroad will run through the county.

YELL

Is situated on the south side of the Arkansas river, having that stream for its northern boundary; population, 8,048. Danville is the county site. Land broken in the south part, in the northern portion river bottoms; soil exceedingly fertile, producing one to one and a half bales of cotton, or sixty to seventy-five bushels of corn to the acre; splendid for stock and fruits; rich in minerals of iron, coal and limestone. The Arkansas river affords facilities for transportation. Dardanelle, with a population of 2,000 is the chief town and the land office for the Clarksville district.

SARBER

Is situated on the south bank of the Arkansas river, west of Yell county; population, 3,764. Boonville is the county site. Land hilly, with valleys and river bottoms; soil rich, producing fine crops of cotton, corn, oats, wheat and hay; good for fruits and stock; timber, oak, hickory, maple and pine; minerals, iron, coal and limestone. The Arkansas river furnishes facilities for shipping to market.

GRANT

Lies between Hot Springs and Jefferson counties; population, 3,943. Sheridan is the county site. Land rolling, with ridges in the western and valleys in the eastern portion; soil rich in the valleys, producing large crops of cotton, corn and hay; rich in minerals; most of the minerals of Hot Springs county extend into this county. The Arkansas and Louisiana railroad will run through the county; and being so near the city of Little Rock, will rapidly increase in population and wealth.

SEBASTIAN

Is situated in the north-west, having the Indian Nation for its western, and the Arkansas river for its northern boundary. It has a population of about thirteen thousand. Fort Smith, the county site, is located on the Arkansas river, at the head of steamboat navigation, and adjoining the government reserve, which lies between it and the Nation. The general character of the land is rolling; prairie, about one third. The soil is very fertile, and well adapted to fruit growing, general farming purposes, and especially for stock raising; as timothy, clover and herds grass grow luxuriantly. The products are, cotton 1 bale, corn 40 to 75 bushels, wheat 10 to 20 bushels, oats 20 to 40 bushels to the acre. Good crops of hay, and Irish, and sweet potatoes are grown. Well adapted to fruit growing, soil and climate are both favorable; those that have orchards are reaping a rich reward, in large crops every year, and big prices. Vegetables of all kinds grow to perfection. In their season, game and fish are abundant, consisting of bear, deer, turkeys, geese, ducks, quails and pigeons, and cat, buffalo, bass, perch, etc.

MINERALS.—Coal is one of the pride products of this county. Several mining villages are in operation, the principal of which, adjoins Jenny Lind, twelve miles from Fort Smith. Coal crops out on the reserve, adjoining Fort Smith; and Mr. Morgan, an English miner, informs me that he has worked in the coal mines of England, Pennsylvania, Ohio, and North Missouri, and that the coal mines of Sebastian county, from what he has seen, give promise of being more extensive and profitable than any he ever worked. There are several companies engaged in mining, hauling the coal to Fort Smith with ox teams, and selling it there at from twenty to twenty-five cents per bushel, and are well satisfied with the profits of the business. What will be the profits when a rail road is running to the mines, and steam power used for hoisting and pumping? At present, every shower drowns out the miners. The late Dr. D. D. Owen, in his Geological Report of Arkansas for the years 1859 and 1860, says: "That the coal fields of Sebastian county, are thicker and more extensive than any in the State; that the coal is one of the most valuable kinds, especially, for manufacturing purposes, and that its quality and thickness must exercise a most important influence on the future prospects of Sebastian county, especially in the location of lines of rail roads in the valley of the Arkansas river."

Timber.—The forest of this county is densely covered by the finest of useful timber, such as oak, black walnut, hickory, gum, cotton wood, cherry, cedar, and yellow pine. The twenty or more saw mills in the county, engaged in sawing lumber to supply the demand for building in Fort Smith, make but a slight impression upon the vast timber resources of the county. The price of lumber in Fort Smith is from seventeen to twenty dollars, at the mills from ten to twelve dollars per thousand feet. Walnut lumber from fifteen to thirty-five dollars per thousand feet.

Rail Roads.—This is a subject in which the people of Fort Smith, and Sebastian county, are deeply interested; and are moving with a determination to have increased facilities, and new routes and connections. There are several important lines of rail roads in embryo.

First, Little Rock and Fort Smith rail road, which we are assured will be completed to Fort Smith by January 1st, 1873.

Second, Fort Smith and Kansas City rail road, with State aid to the amount of $15,000 per mile. This road will run from Fort Smith, through Crawford, Washington and Benton counties to the Missouri line, there connecting with the Kansas city branch. We are told by the directors of the road, that the money is ready to build and complete it in eighteen months from date. It runs through some of the finest grain, stock, and fruit growing lands of north-west Arkansas, and will be of great advantage to Sebastian county and north-west Arkansas, giving rail facilities to a market north for early fruits, vegetables, stock, coal, lumber, timber, and other products. It is also contemplated to extend it south, through the coal and timber region, to Jefferson, and Galveston, Texas. This road will add more to the wealth and population of Fort Smith and

Sebastian county, than any of the projected rail roads in the county.

The Atlantic and Pacific, and Missouri, Kansas and Texas rail roads are each compelled, by their charters, to build branches from their main lines, in the nation, to Fort Smith, connecting at the latter place with the Little Rock and Fort Smith rail road. These branch roads will most likely be built this year. There are also two or three other rail roads chartered through the county, which will most likely be built in time.

City of Fort Smith.—In 1816, a rangers' post was established on what is now the government reserve, and was called Fort Smith. In 1837, the land immediately adjoining on the north-east, was laid out as a town and named city of Fort Smith. The site is a beautiful one, the land rising gradually from the river, amid the hills and dales, the picturesque grandeur of the Arkansas river in full view for miles, gives to the city a favorable position as you approach from the river. The business portion of the city is principally constructed of brick and stone, and embraces some handsome blocks, which will compare favorably, in point of solidity and architectural beauty, with St. Louis or Chicago business blocks. The business is mostly done on Garrison avenue, a wide street, and from early morn till dewy eve, that wide avenue is crowded with teams from the surrounding country, with the various products of the country.

The outskirts of the city are lined with gardens, where the pointed gables of elegant villas rise through the trees. Some of them cost as high as $10,000, and compare favorably with any in the State. In the manufacturing line there is one large flouring mill complete, two cotton gins, two grist mills, two saw mills, one planing mill, one foundry and machine shop, two breweries, two wagon manufactories. In churches, there are neat buildings of the following denominations: Catholic, Baptist, Lutheran, Episcopal, Methodist, Presbyterian, Christian, Methodist (colored), and Baptist (colored); all with respectable congregations. In the school line, it has a Catholic female school, Lutheran and Baptist schools, and three public schools, one of which is for colored people. There are five newspapers, two of them tri-weekly and weekly, the rest weekly. The United States court for the western district of Arkansas, is held at Fort Smith. At the close of the war, the city contained a population of 1,700, which now exceeds 5,000, another evidence that it is no slow town. The people are possessed with more than ordinary energy, and have no idea of being left behind in the commercial race with the cities through this great section of country.

Fort Smith is destined to become a large manufacturing place, surrounded by forests of valuable timber, and situated in the lap of the rich and inexhaustible coal fields of Sebastian county. She presents inducements to the capitalist that few places offer, to effect a junction of the manufacturer and consumer, without the cost of transportation. She will also become a great lumber market for distributing the sawed product of the forest immediately surrounding, to her less favored sister cities of the plains west, and north-west. Five years hence will find Fort Smith a large manufacturing and lumber dealing city, with rail roads running east, north, west, and one running south through the rich mineral and timber regions of the western border of the State. The business men of Fort Smith are public spirited, enterprising and wide awake, liberally encouraging every enterprise likely to benefit not only the city, but the whole country; and the rapid growth of Fort Smith shows the most gratifying results.

CITY OF LITTLE ROCK.

The city of Little Rock is situated, geographically, very nearly in the center of the State, on the south side of the Arkansas river, in the center of Pulaski county; built upon a high, rolling plain overlooking the Arkansas river and surrounding country for miles in every direction. The healthfulness of the place has long been established, the drainage being natural and excellent. As you approach the city, its appearance is impressive; located on high land with an easy grade to the river, the spires of the churches pointing heavenward in every portion of the city, suggestive of morality, and the houses, surrounded by shrubbery and evergreen magnolia trees, stand like gems in a well kept garden. The location is one of the finest imaginable. From the roof of the State House, the eye falls upon a landscape of marvelous beauty and vast extent. From the northwest comes the Arkansas, winding its course past the city on towards the southeast, and for miles to the south stretches vast fertile lands, diversified by gentle hills and healthful ridges, and to the north may be seen well cultivated fields and substantial farm houses, giving to the scene a civilized appearance.

Little Rock is not only the geographical but the commercial center of the State, and promises to grow rapidly into a large and important place. It is located at a point on the river which steamboats can always reach; is the terminus of several railroads, and the centre of several more, and will be to Arkansas and the southwest what Chicago is to Illinois and the northwest; the largest commercial, manufacturing and important city, located in the heart of a country rich in minerals and forest, surrounded by rich and fertile soil, and at an early day to be connected with every city and harbor in the United States. The facilities to become the great distributing point for a vast inland country, are not equaled by any other place in the southwest. Its manufacturing interests are well looked after and encouraged, and are rapidly enlarging. Judging from what has been accomplished in establishing manufactories during the past few years, Little Rock is destined to become the principal manufacturing city of the southwest. Every natural advantage that may be wished to support manufactories, are found here. Coal of the best quality is abundant. Improvements are continually being made; extensive and substantial business houses are rapidly building, to accommodate its fast increasing trade; elegant and attractive dwelling houses are appearing in all parts of the city; large and beautiful churches and school houses are to be seen all over the city, and everything being done to improve and beautify the place. Built on a series of hills, she enjoys a beautiful prospect of the surrounding country, besides receiving the full benefit of the pleasant, invigorating and healthful breezes; to the beholder, at a distance, she presents a fine and attractive appearance.

The opening out of new channels to trade, and the development of the resources of our city and State, have made rapid strides within the past three years. Almost daily some new enterprise is brought to light, and the people of Little Rock were never more wide awake to their interests than they have been of late. Not only have several new lines of railroads been recently projected to Little Rock, but other and equally important forward movements are being made. The city is well built and has a prosperous business air; her people have confidence in the future; it has never had any fictitious or unhealthy growth; "For Rent" and "For sale" are not the signs painted on many houses; on the contrary, it is difficult to find a vacant house.

Little Rock is the most beautiful city in the State; its streets are all broad and at right angles with each other. Her business houses are for the most part of brick, handsome storehouses and substantial warehouses, filled with large stocks of goods. Land being plenty and cheap, the residences are not crowded together, but attached to each house is a garden and yard, where fruit and shade trees thrive, and blooms the famed magnolia tree with its broad green leaves and snow white flowers. The mild winters enable its residents to indulge in many choice shrubs, vines and flowers that are too tender for the northern States.

Little Rock, though in its infancy, is quite a large city; has a flourishing business appearance, and growing rapidly every day. On every street are signs of activity and business; over twelve hundred houses, costing nearly three million dollars, have been constructed during the last year. Twenty-odd large storehouses and several residences, all of brick, and costing from $5,000 to $35,000 each, are now being erected. Of churches, there are fine buildings of the following denominations: Episcopal, Presbyterian, Methodist, Catholic, Lutheran, Baptist, Christian, Methodist (colored) and Baptist (colored.) The churches are well sustained and well attended, and we can say that in Little Rock there are all those peculiar elements that go to build up a good moral community.

In the school line, "Little Rock contains several good schools of a high grade. Prominent among these is St. John's college, a Masonic institution, with collegiate charter and powers. Though discontinued during the war, it resumed soon after, and is again in a flourishing condition. Saint Mary's Academy, for girls and young ladies, in charge of the Sisters of the Convent of Mercy. This never suspended operation during the war, and is in a prosperous condition. In addition, there are more than a dozen public schools, well taught and graded, in some of which, at least, pupils can be prepared for any college in the land." The educational institutions of the city are excellent. The State has made very liberal provisions for the education of the youth of every color, sex and condition.

NEWSPAPERS.

There are three newspapers, daily and weekly—the *Republican* and *Journal*, both Republican, and the *Gazette*, Democratic; also a monthly paper, the *Educational Journal*; neutral in politics, devoted to the educational interest of the country.

AMUSEMENTS.

Little Rock, although crowded with churches, is not averse to lighter amusements. It has several large halls, finely lighted and ventilated, for lectures, concerts and theatricals.

BANKS.

There are three or four banks and several insurance companies here, all doing a safe and lucrative business.

The Free Masons have a Commandery, Council, Chapter and Lodge organized; the Odd-Fellows have their Encampment and Lodge.

In the hotel line, Little Rock has several good hotels, whose tables are supplied with every thing the market affords, with rooms well furnished, ventilated and aired. In addition, there are a great number of fine, well kept boarding houses, under the management of accomplished ladies, who make their guests feel at home, either in the parlor or dining room.

In the legal line, Little Rock is second to no place in the southwest, having acquired a reputation long since for the eminent legal ability of her lawyers.

Under the judicious management of the City Council, the financial affairs of the city are in a most flattering condition, her scrip selling for ninety-nine cents on the dollar and passing at par all over the State.

Her wharf is equal to any on the Mississippi river (except St. Louis and New Orleans) and is now being greatly enlarged.

The principal business streets are Markham and Main which will compare well with Fourth and Fifth streets, St. Louis. They are now in process of paving with wood. The city is lighted with gas, and the sidewalks are sentineled with maple and catalpa trees. Her business men are active and reliable, doing a safe and profitable business. There are more than a dozen wholesale houses selling goods to all parts of the State accessible by the present means of conveyance; and judging by the private residences of the business men, selling goods, wares and merchandise has been a profitable business in Little Rock, for the buildings are mostly of a substantial character, betokening wealth and taste on the part of the owners.

LITTLE ROCK WATER WORKS COMPANY.

A chartered company, to supply the city with water on the Holly system. The estimated cost of the works necessary to furnish an ample supply is $150,000, to be completed within three years.

STREET RAIL ROAD COMPANY.

Incorporated under the general incorporation laws of the State. The company expect to have several miles of railway in operation this year; and that portion from the city to the fair grounds is expected to be ready for travel by October, at which time the annual State Fair is held, which will be a great stimulus to the Fair Association, rendering travel to and from the grounds easy, rapid and cheap.

IN THE MANUFACTURING LINE,

There are the Little Rock Manufacturing Company, that takes the logs, saws, planes and manufactures sash, blinds, doors, frames, mouldings, scroll and ornamental sawing. In addition, there are three more planing mills that make sash, doors, blinds, frames, etc. Two saw mills in the city, and fourteen in the county, that are kept running day and night to supply the demand for lumber in Little Rock. Two first class flouring mills; two iron founderies and machine shops; one marble tomb stone establishment; one rectifying establishment; two wagon factories; and the State Manufacturing Company at the Penitentiary, where persons who have made themselves obnoxious to their fellow men, are confined within its walls, ornamented with a suit of Zebra clothing, and put to work making wagons, furniture, brick, etc.; and under the excellent management of the State administration, these parties cost the State but a trifle in comparison with the same institutions of other States.

LITTLE ROCK AS A COMMERCIAL CITY.

Situated as she is, in the midst of the greatest producing and consuming region of the State, and destined at a very early day to be connected by rail with every portion of the State, and every city and port of the United States; with a vast country directly tributary, gives her more natural advantages, to become a large commercial city and distributing point, than any city in the south-west. Her projected rail roads penetrate the richest regions of the State, and the south-west; and the amount of trade they will ultimately bring to Little Rock, as the country becomes more closely settled up, will insure the building up of a large commercial city. Her situation is most admirable to control and command the trade of Arkansas and the country west and south, and we may further add, that the business men of Little Rock are fully alive to their interest, and the important position of Little Rock, and liberally encourage every enterprise likely to benefit not only Little Rock, but the whole State. Every day her streets are crowded with wagons and people from a long distance in all directions, and her business houses present that stirring, active appearance indicative of brisk business. Her trade during the past season has been much larger up to this time than during any corresponding period in the past. Large quantities of cotton, grain, and other products are daily coming in; money is plenty, and everything is conducive to a brisk and healthy business.

In addition to her commercial interest, it is evident to the close observer, that Little Rock will become a great

MANUFACTURING CITY.

Little Rock enjoys great natural advantages to become a large manufacturing city. Situated in the center of the State, in the heart of the mineral wealth of the State, on a river that furnishes unlimited water power and transportation, and in addition, the rail roads now building to and centering at Little Rock, will bring her in direct connection with the rich coal, iron, lead, and other minerals, which have heretofore been shut out from a market and closed against capital and industry. The valuable timber of which this whole State abounds in, will find a ready market. The coal, which now lies unmined, will be rapidly taken out, and brought to Little Rock, for supplying the great number of manufacturing establishments that will be operated here, by reason of the facilities for cheap transportation afforded. This place seems to have attracted the attention of the reading men, at least, of the United States, judging by the way active men have invested in real estate, and opened business houses of all kinds in the last two years. Here is an opening for capital and skilled labor. The three things which determine whether a town is so located as to be able to *build* up manufacturing interest on an extensive scale, are here in abundance and for all time.

First, Facilities for cheap and ready transportation. Little Rock is centrally located in the State, in the Arkansas valley, on the Arkansas river, which furnishes water transportation at least ten months of the twelve in the year, to the outside world, from Pittsburg to New Orleans, from Saint Paul to St. Louis. Then by rail, in a short time, to all parts of the country, north, south, east and west. Thus it will be seen that Little Rock has facilities for cheap and ready transportation to and from all parts of the country. History shows that all large manufacturing and commercial cities are located on navigable water courses. Cities so located, having also rail road facilities, have a great advantage over cities in the interior, with equal rail road facilities. Water courses will always furnish the cheapest road bed for heavy freights, and serve as an equalizer of commercial rates of transportation.

Second, An abundant supply near at hand of the raw material entering into the manufactured products. The location of Little Rock, in the center of the rich mineral and metal resources, and in the midst of the finest timbered section of the Union, surrounded by forests of oak, ash, black walnut, pine etc., which densely cover the uncleared lands of Arkansas, invite the erection of manufactories for the production of every article that can be made from metal and wood. Here are inducements which cannot long be overlkooed by capital, and the enterprising people of the country.

Third, Fuel, the coal basin of Arkansas extends from below Little Rock, on both sides of the river to the western limits of the State at Fort Smith. There is a wide region immediately surrounding and west of Little Rock, undoubtedly underlaid with coal through its whole extent, only worked in few places, and this where there were visible outcrops; which is proof sufficient, that Little Rock has fuel for all time and of the best quality. It is a well known fact that most of the great manufacturing cities of the country have but one or two of these indispensible elements of special advantage. Now what shall be said of the prospects of the city of Little Rock, that has them all in abundance?

The mineral resources of the State, lying immediately around Little Rock, consisting of iron, lead, copper, zinc, etc., will make her the Pittsburg of Arkansas. Here will be located furnaces, founderies, rolling mills, machine shops, car building shops, and all manner of factories. In more than half the counties of the State, may be found valuable minerals, and in illimitable quantities. The example of Pennsylvania shows how prosperous a people may become who will manufacture their ores. By this means we will not only retain within our borders the money of which we are now depleted, but build up a home market for our farmers, and the greater will be our ability to possess the comforts and luxuries of life. When mining enterprises are founded, as they will assuredly be, in a short time contiguous to rivers and lines of rail roads, the tillers of the soil will reap rich rewards, lands will advance in value, and golden harvests will be gathered by the agriculturist. Towns and villages will spring into existence, and mechanics, artisans, and laborers of whatsoever kind will be benefitted. Verily there is a new era dawning for Arkansas; and the city of Little Rock, located precisely in the geographical center of Arkansas, is destined to become the most important city in the south-west; none can doubt who study its commanding position and unrivalled advantages, situated in the center of the famous Arkansas valley, the most magnificent region in the south; a valley alone sufficient to sustain a population of two million inhabitants, whose wants, likewise, would sustain a population in Little Rock of at least three hundred thousand inhabitants. And, think at what *nominal prices* lots in Little Rock can now be bought, which in a few years must become very valuable.

In addition to her agricultural, commercial and manufacturing interests, there can be no question but that Little Rock is to become one of the great

RAILROAD CENTERS

Of the southwest, and one of the "future great cities of the country." By reference to the map of the United States, you will see that the position of Little Rock and the railroads already built and those under construction, gives to her position a far better prospect to become a great railroad center than any other city in the southwest.

We now proceed to set forth her great system of railroads, completed, constructing and projected, coming into Little Rock from the north side of the river:

1. Memphis and Little Rock Railroad.—Completed. This is an important road, giving us connection at Memphis with all the cities of the south and east. Being the only completed railroad from the east, it is crowded with business. It runs through a rich agricultural country.

2. Little Rock and Fort Smith Railroad.—Cars running sixty miles west of Little Rock; fifty miles more ready for the iron, and the rest—forty miles—grubbed and chopped out. When completed, this road will be an important line, connecting at Fort Smith with a branch of the Atlantic and Pacific, from near the Canadian river, and then on through to California. This is one of our Pacific railroads, and by this road we will receive our teas and silks from the East Indies. With a country of wonderful mineral and other wealth to develop, together with its western connections, will make it, when completed, one of the great through lines connecting the west with the east.

3. *Arkansas Central Railroad.*—From Helena, on the Mississippi, to Little Rock, with a branch from Aberdeen, where it crosses White river, to Pine Bluff. This is an important road, giving us connection at Helena with the Helena and Mobile railroad to Mobile, Alabama, one of the great cotton and coffee ports of the United States, and under the management of its energetic and experienced railroad president, Colonel Dorsey, is progressing rapidly towards completion. The iron has arrived from Europe, and the rolling stock from St. Louis. This road runs through a fine agricultural country.

4. *Cairo and Fulton Railroad.*—From Cairo, Illinois, to Little Rock. This is one of the grandest railroad enterprises in the southwest, giving us railroad connection with St. Louis, Chicago and the east; and under the management of Colonel Thomas Allen, the railroad king of Missouri, and his associates, is being rapidly pushed to completion, and is under contract to be running cars into Little Rock by July 1st, 1872. This road runs through a country rich in soil, minerals and timber.

5. *St. Louis, Iron Mountain and Little Rock Railroad.*—From St. Louis, via. Iron Mountain railroad, to Little Rock. Of the three hundred and forty miles necessary to connect Little Rock and St. Louis, two hundred and six miles are in operation, and one hundred and thirty-four miles being graded. The work is under contract to be completed and the cars running from St. Louis to Little Rock by the first day of July, 1872. This is another of Colonel Thomas Allen's roads; and judging from the expeditious work thus far, we feel assured that

the line will be completed by next July. This road will be of immense advantage to Little Rock, by reason of cheap freights to and from the north, and passing through a country rich in minerals and other wealth.

6. *St. Louis and Little Rock Railroad.*--From St. Louis via. Atlantic and Pacific Railroad, to Cuba station, Crawford county, Missouri; thence direct through Batesville, on White river, to Little Rock. This is an important road to Little Rock, bringing to this city an immense trade from north Arkansas that now finds its way to Memphis, down White river. The counties through which this road runs are rich in minerals and agriculture. Several hundred hands are now at work and considerable track laid. The Jefferson City and Little Rock railroad will probably unite with this road at Cuba station and run cars to Little Rock. This road also gives us connection at Batesville with the Memphis and Kansas City railroad, and by that road with the Kansas Pacific and Union Pacific railroad to California.

Now cross the river and we find the following railroads constructing and projected into Little Rock:

1. *Little Rock, Pine Bluff and New Orleans Railroad*, under the able and successful management of Col. James M. Lewis, its president. This road is being rapidly constructed in a substantial manner to its terminus at Eunice, on the Mississippi, distance one hundred and sixty miles. Eighty-two miles are graded, bridged and furnished with cross ties; twenty miles of track is laid, and iron purchased for forty miles more. In addition, the rolling stock and engines, ample for the road, have been purchased and a part have arrived. The road, as regards grades, bridges, cross ties, buildings and machinery, is fully up to the requirements of a first class road. When this road is completed, it will be difficult to over estimate the benefit to the city and the counties through which it runs. This road will not only add immensely to the growth and wealth of Little Rock, but will also give shorter and more direct communication from St. Louis and Little Rock to New Orleans, and Little Rock being nearly equi-distant from St. Louis and

New Orleans, gives her an important position. The cotton and other products of the rich counties through which it runs will be consigned to Little Rock, to be shipped to New York; and over this road we can import at low rates all our sugar, molasses, rice, oranges and other tropical fruits.

2. *Cairo and Fulton Railroad.*—This road extends from the south side of the river, in Little Rock, through Arkadelphia to Fulton, on Red river; thence to Marshal, Texas, and on through Texas to the Rio Grande, at Laredo. This is called the International railroad, and is one of the grandest railroad enterprises in the country, connecting the north with the gulf of Mexico. By this road we connect with the Texas Pacific at Marshal; intersect with every railroad in, and penetrates the richest portion of Texas. This road is under contract to be completed to Fulton by January 1, 1874, and is another of Colonel Thomas Allen's roads, which is a sufficient guarantee that it will be hurried on to completion and its equipments first class. This road not only gives us connection with the Queen city of the west, St. Louis, but with every railroad and city in Texas; and the richly ladened cars over the Texas Pacific, with their freight from the East Indies, will drag their long lengths through our city to the northeast. This road, also, will be the most direct route from St. Louis and Chicago to Texas.

3. *Little Rock and Shreveport Railroad*, from Little Rock, via. Princeton, Camden and Magnolia to Shreveport, there connecting with the railroad system of Louisiana and Texas. This road will run through a section of the State remarkably rich in agriculture, the Ouachita and Red river country, where from one to two bales of cotton are produced to the acre—a section whose local traffic alone would sustain a railroad, to say nothing of the through business by reason of the connections at Shreveport, which will be immense. This road and the Cairo and Fulton road will bring to Little Rock the trade of a scope of country eighty miles wide by three hundred miles in length, extending to the center of Texas, a country that is naturally tributary to Little Rock. Now, granting these con-

siderations, which I presume all will grant to be true in the general if not in the particular as unqualifiedly as I have presented it, then certainly Little Rock has as much to expect from these two roads as any other two centering within her limits, and her business men should use all possible means to further their early completion, for with proper facilities furnished, the whole trade of that country could be secured to Little Rock. And further, now is the time for the Cairo and Fulton and Little Rock and Shreveport railroads to put forth their best energies, and push the work to the earliest possible conclusion. The country through which they will run gives promise of far greater prosperity than ever before. Large additions will be made to the areas devoted to agriculture, furnishing remunerative employment to an army of laborers, and augmenting the bulk of local produce to be marketed abroad to an extent that will tax the freight capacity of both roads, besides the through business that will seek a market over these roads. Additional facilities always create increased business; there will be plenty of business for both roads.

4. Arkansas and Louisiana Rail Road.—From Little Rock via. Alexander, Opelousas, and Berwick's Bay to New Orleans, running through a fertile and rich mineral country.

5. The Hot Springs and Little Rock Rail Road.—From Little Rock to Hot Springs, distance 60 miles. When this road is completed the Hot Springs, now justly celebrated, will become a place of great resort; and the crystal mountains of Montgomery county, will be within easy access.

6. Arkansas Central Rail Road.—From Little Rock west to the Indian Nation, and on through the Nation. This will run through counties rich in agriculture and peculiarly rich in minerals.

Thus we have twelve distinct trunk roads, converging at Little Rock, built, under way of construction, and projected, and not one will be abandoned. What other city in the south west will have so many, or likely to be favored with so great a number? The building of all these lines of rail roads is an assured fact, and they will be of incalculable benefit to us, important to the country, even if they did not pass through a region of unexampled richness in soil, timber, coal, iron, lead, etc. Arkansas is building a net-work of rail roads extending all through the land, and centering at Little Rock, from every part of the State, the rapid development of which, she sees close at hand, and the unspeakable value of whose trade she recognizes, and seeks to make her own; binding its people to Little Rock in bonds of mutual interest, and thus build up a trade which will grow more valuable and extensive as the years roll on; and the tide of fortune will roll in to enrich our city, build its banks, marble palaces and beautify its suburbs. The people of Little Rock fully realize that the splendid system of rail roads laid out in Arkansas, will give us direct rail connection with all parts of the world; and the extra opportunities Arkansas offers the immigrant to establish himself among us are not excelled by any other State.

The following statement of distances will show how Little Rock stands in relation to some of the principal cities of the country:

	Places.	Miles.
From Little Rock to	St Louis	340
" Little Rock to	Galveston	510
" Little Rock to	New Orleans	410
" Little Rock to	San Deigo, Cal	1,600
" Little Rock to	Laredo	700
" Little Rock to	Memphis	131
" Little Rock to	Mobile	471
" Little Rock to	New York	1,000

POPULATION CONSIDERED.

"The first essential want of any productive people is markets, whereat to dispose of their surplus products, mechanical or agricultural, at profitable prices. Markets are a want of population in all lands. Population alone adds value to lands and property of every kind, and is therefore, one of the principal sources and causes of wealth, because it creates a market by causing a demand for property and products; it enhances their price and value, rewards the producer for his industry, and encourages and increases industry and production. Population thus creates markets."

Pulaski county, in which Little Rock is located, stood ninth in point of population, as compared with the other counties in the State. Now it contains more than double the inhabitants of any other county in the State, owing mainly to the beauty and healthfulness of the location of Little Rock, and the splendid agricultural region, lying above and below it on the river.

No one will need be told that though Little Rock escaped any considerable damage in the way of destruction during the war, that all growth stopped from 1861 to 1866. In fact, no marked or rapid revival of growth began until 1867, since when it has made most rapid progress. In

	1850	1860	1865	1870
Little Rock had a population of.......	2,167...	3,727....	4,000...	14,000

And to-day, contains between eighteen thousand and twenty thousand people. The city now covers four times the area, and contains more than four times the population and wealth it did ten years ago, with every prospect and reason to hope that ten years hence, will find it with more than four times as much of both as now.

From its present and future prospects, we have no hesitation in placing the population of Little Rock in 1880 at between 50,000 and 60,000 people, and in the year 1890, 100,000 inhabitants. Little Rock is also the headquarters for all parties going to or coming from the Hot Springs, 60 miles south-west; which are widely celebrated for their curative properties, especially rheumatism or nervous affections.

Little Rock, in addition to being the geographical, agricultural, commercial, manufacturing and rail road center, is also the *political center* of the State. Here are located all the buildings belonging to and necessary for running the machinery of the State government. And as a matter of course people from all parts of the State have more or less business at the capital and central city, thereby not only spending thousands of dollars, but necessitating the completion of all the rail roads centering at Little Rock, which, when in operation, must necessarily become the grand thoroughfares for the vast commerce and travel between the east and west, north and south. The through trade would be of immense benefit to Little Rock, and of great consequence would be the opening up of the magnificent country through which the road would run, and of which Little Rock must become the trading center. A costly and magnificent bridge is now being constructed across the river at Little Rock, to connect the system of rail roads converging at Little Rock. When this connection is made, Little Rock will indeed be one of the chief rail road centers of the Union, with unequaled facilities for receiving and distributing the travel and productions which must concentrate at that point. · Little Rock is situated almost on the 35th parallel, and with the completion of the 35th parallel rail way, the most feasable and practicable route for a trans-continental rail road, will be directly on the world's thoroughfare, and from her geographical position, would control a great portion of the future vast trans-continental trade and travel, by becoming an important point upon the "world's highway."

The State Agricultural and Mechanical Fair Association, is also located at Little Rock. This Association was organized in 1867, with a capital stock of $20,000, in shares of ten dollars each. In 1869 the Association reorganized under the general corporation laws of 1868, and the shares were put at $25 00 each. The fair grounds embrace a forty acre tract, costing $4,000, and upon the grounds have been expended over $10,000 in improvements.

THE PUBLIC BUILDINGS,

Are the capitol, with the east and west wings, in which are the offices of the Governor, Hon. O. A. Hadley; Hon. Henry Page, Treasurer; the Auditor, to whom application must be made for donation lands; and Hon. James M. Lewis, Commissioner of Immigration and State Lands, who will always be glad to give information or assistance to immigrants; and who also has, by law, entire control of all the lands owned by the State, except the school, or sixteenth section lands; and all applications to purchase must be made to his office. The Superintendent of Public Instruction has charge of the school lands. The Blind Assylum, the Deaf and Dumb Institute, and the Penitentiary. A city of churches truly is this place, costly and splendid edifices, presided over by ministers who possess more than ordinary ability. Its school houses are substantial buildings. The principal educational establishment, however, is St. John's College, a substantial brick edifice, presenting a very imposing appearance. From the great variety and rare beauty of the flowers and shrubs in the public and private gardens, Little Rock has long been known as the "City of Roses," or "Flower City."

Little Rock is a young city, just beginning to grow into notice; yet its assessed value of real estate for 1871 foots up $8,709,475, and in the additions to the city, $160,529. In ten years from date, the real and personal taxable property of Little Rock will reach $50,000,000. Mark the prediction!

Since 1867, the increase in population and wealth have been nearly 400 per cent. and the causes and influences now at work, will make the growth more rapid in the next ten years than ever in the past. Hence we regard it as reasonable to claim that its prospects for continued growth are better than at any time in the past.

WANTS OF ARKANSAS.

Capital that shall be active, labor that shall be judiciously employed, and population that shall possess the land, cultivate the soil and develop the resources of the State. The resources of the State in metals and minerals are yet imperfectly known by the outside world, and, of course, still more imperfectly developed. When they become more fully understood, the claim of Arkansas to become the empire State of the southwest will be more generally admitted, because it will be seen that her admirable position, her present wealth and growing enterprises will enable her to command capital for her numerous needs for all time to come, which will bring in its train prosperity to all sections and increased development of the wealth of the State. A diversification of the industry of her people.

The State has abundant water power, extensive coal fields, inexhaustible mines of metals and minerals, and forests of the best timber known in mechanical uses. Manufactories should be established; cotton and woolen fabrics should be made at home, and especially should her timber be manufactured into furniture, wagons, carriages, plows, and every article that can be made from wood; tanneries, for making leather; soap, for washing clothes; factories for manufacturing tobacco; iron works, for making iron; founderies, for making castings; furnaces, for smelting lead ore; lime kilns for burning lime and a great many other manufactories for making hundreds of articles of every day use, to procure which she now sends her money abroad; and those very articles can be manufactured at home cheaper than the foreign article can be sold for here. Heretofore the material sources of wealth have been mostly neglected. Arkansas, too, must foster and encourage immigration, having superior inducements for immigrants from other States and from Europe to push into this State with the same enterprise that now leads them to the northwest, even to the far off snow clad line of the Northern Pacific railway. The time is near at hand when all these elements of material greatness may be possessed by Arkansas, which have made other and less favored States rich whilst Arkansas, with resources and advantages excelled by none and equaled by few, has been for years comparatively at a stand still.

Did the northwestern States, of unlimited area and cheapness of land, complacently fold their arms and wait for capital and immigration to voluntarily come in and create such cities as Chicago, Milwaukie, Kansas City and other wealthy places? No; they, with a true appreciation of the importance and value of immigration, calculated means commensurate with the undertaking. So must Arkansas, if she desires her resources to be developed; and in proportion to the more extended development of her resources, will the taxable wealth of the State be increased and individual taxation be reduced; and, also, more abundant will be the income to meet taxation. The pressure of population and the demand for land will not only increase the value of lands, but will demand the full development of the varied resources of the State, thereby creating a market at home for all, alike to the miner, mechanic, manufacturer and farmer, which will enable all to reap the full and undivided benefits that would accrue.

In the next ten years we may anticipate an immense improvement. The extension of railroad facilities is constantly enlarging the area of farming, mineral and timber lands that are immediately available for the production of the people's wants. We raise the cotton and sell it to New England and old England for fifteen cents per pound, then buy it back, in the form of prints and domestics, at from twelve to thirty cents per yard, when a pound of cotton will make three yards of cloth, and the climate of the State affords a better temperature necessary to be maintained in cotton mills than in either of the above countries. The two things required for cotton manufacturing is capital and cheap labor; the labor we have, the capital we want. Woolen factories especially should be built here, where we can raise the raw material in superabundance. Furniture, wagon, carriage, plow, and other wood working factories could be successfully maintained in every third county in the State. We send to Cincinnati for our furniture, where walnut lumber is worth $65 per thousand, whilst here it is worth from $15 to $30. We send to Illinois and Wisconsin for farm wagons, and to New York and New Hampshire for carriages, when the whole State abounds with the best of timber used in their manufacture; even our ax, hoe, rake, fork and broom handles come from Ohio. We send our beef hides east to be manipulated into leather, when the barks sumach, etc., necessary for tanning purposes, are here in abundance. We even send to St. Louis and Cincinnati for washing soap, and with the order for soap, we send the tallow, at six cents per pound, to make it. Soil and climate just suited for tobacco culture, producing 2,225,000 pounds in the State, in 1869, averaging 666 pounds to the acre, and scarcely a tobacco factory in the State. We send to Pennsylvania and even old England for iron, when we have inexhaustible beds of iron ore in various portions of the State, and that, too, as at Spadra, the best in the world, carbonate ore, same as the Staffordshire, England, iron ore. Our castings come from St. Louis and Pittsburg. We have as rich lead mines as there are in the United States, and that, too, surrounded by a rich agricultural country. We have immense quarries of the best limestone for burning lime; but send off to Louisville, Kentucky, and to Alabama for lime, which costs us from three to four dollars per barrel. We send to New York and Ohio for our cheese and a great portion of our butter, costing the consumers here twenty-five to thirty-five cents for cheese and forty to sixty cents for butter. I believe there is not a cheese factory in the State. Home produced butter, white and crumbly as a snow ball, will bring twenty cents in summer and from forty to fifty cents in winter. I am positive that in no other State will butter and cheese making pay as well as here, with the best of grass land and a climate that precludes the necessity of shelter or winter feeding, and a home market in every county, or at the thriving and commercial center, Little Rock, which will soon be connected with every portion of the State by river or rail. While grocery stores throughout the State have placarded advertisements of Ohio, New York and creamery butter, excellent butter is made by individuals all over the State, but not enough to supply one-twentieth of the demand. In fact, good butter is difficult to obtain, even at any price, all through the year. In addition to the wild grass, all the valuable tame grasses produce a luxuriant growth; the water is good, clear and cold, the night air is cool, cows are cheap, land is cheap, and every thing needful to enable the manufacturer of butter and cheese to produce a good article and reap a rich harvest.

Only capitalists, skilled laborers and a million of enterprising farmers are wanting to make Arkansas one of the richest and most powerful States of the Mississippi valley. It is a land full of the raw material for manufacturers, undeveloped mines of metals and minerals that exceed in richness and extent the mines of most any other section, only awaiting the hand of capital and skilled labor to yield their untold millions of wealth; a country scarce of tenants, with rich bottoms, fruitful ridges and broad table lands, traversed by meandering streams, presenting unbroken acres to the thrifty farmer; a country as beautiful as God ever made, seems waiting and inviting immigrants to come and take possession.

RAIL ROAD WANTS.

These very necessary and important internal improvements towards developing the resources of the State, we are gratified to say are making rapid progress. Many circumstances have taken place since the war, to retard and prevent the rapid construction of the rail roads of the State until within the last year or two, chiefly among the causes, was the poverty, not only of the State, but the people, rendered by the devastation of the war fiend; and for four or five years after the war closed, the people had no time or money to devote to rail road building. But within the last year or two, the people having recuperated to a certain extent their losses, and having taken a survey of the north-western States, see that rail roads have been the means of developing the resources, causing manufacturing operations to be established, building up cities and increasing the wealth and population of other States of the Union, and consequently, would do the same thing in Arkansas. Therefore, the people and also the State, have shown marked liberality in State aid, and local subscription of bonds, money, and lands to rail road companies, and as a consequence, in no other State are rail roads projected and building with such rapid strides as in Arkansas. The rail road necessities of the State will soon be ample to afford to all portions, facilities for travel and shipment to the markets of the world. Incalculable benefits will speedily follow the completion of the rail road lines now being constructed in the State. Arkansas, by reason of her situation in the most favored parallels of latitude, and her wonderful rich resources of mines, soils and timber, should be and is, the most attractive State in the Union; and it only needs the completion of the splendid system of rail roads at present inaugurated, to bring into the State, the other wants, namely, capital, skilled laborers, and enterprising farmers. Certainly no other State can offer greater inducements to capitalists, for no other State possesses the useful minerals to a larger extent or greater variety, and those same mineral lands can now be bought for extremely low prices, which in a few years will become very valuable.

Agricultural and fruit lands can be purchased now for five dollars per acre, which in less time than five years, will be worth twenty dollars. Now if it pays a farmer in Iowa to raise corn and sell it at thirty cents, wheat at eighty cents, oats at twenty cents, potatoes at forty cents per bushel, cabbage at five cents per head, etc., should it not pay farmers in Arkansas most handsomely, when there is a good and lasting market, for corn eighty cents wheat one dollar and fifty cents, oats seventy-five cents, potatoes one to two dollars per bushel, and cabbage at twenty to thirty cents a head, and every thing else at the same rate; and that too, when the soil and climate are both more favorable to their growth, and the quality equally as good. Is not this fact suggestive of the superior inducements that Arkansas affords to immigrants? It cannot be claimed that the soil of Arkansas is not adapted to the growing of grains or vegetables, for we have seen a ten acre field of wheat yield three hundred and ten bushels of beautiful grain; a twenty acre field of corn, yield on an average, seventy bushels to the acre. Potatoes have measured up three hundred bushels to the acre; and larger cabbage, onions, beets, etc., are not raised anywhere else, unless on the volcanic soils of Colorado or Calafornia.

Everything is, in Arkansas, favorable to a system of grain and vegetable farming; and as for fruit growing or stock raising, the soil and climate are more favorable than any other State in the Mississippi valley, and we think in the Union. These are all facts that have been demonstrated, and not wordy puffs from interested parties. To the skeptical we simply say come and see for yourself.

ADVICE TO IMMIGRANTS.

I am satisfied, from personal observations, that the great and manifold advantages Arkansas offers to the emigrants from other States, and from Europe, are not equalled by any other State in the Union, and that they may be made known to the outside world, I have endeavored to speak truthfully and plainly of a few of the many advantages that Arkansas possesses, without any desire to boast over any other States, but as a fact susceptible of demonstration. But let no one come to Arkansas, thinking he can gather gold from the top of the ground, or pick greenbacks from the trees. This is a good country for a lazy man, but we have quite enough of that class already. We want immigrants that will go to work with an earnestness to accomplish something for themselves; and in no other part of the Union, will their labor be better rewarded. And the best evidence we have of that is, that those who have come, are quite contented with the country, and are rapidly accumulating a competence. Success anywhere, depends quite as much upon the man as upon the country. Some men will flourish where others would starve! and it is difficult to put such under circumstances where they will not make a living. Unless one has made up his mind to be pleased, he had better make a visit here and see for himself. Immigrants coming in the spring, if in February or March, have ample time to put in a crop, as corn can be planted from March until the first of June. And they will have no trouble in renting land, for in every county there are a great number of farms, and cleared land to rent, with good buildings, water, timber and other things needful, convenient. And there is not a county in the State, where unimproved land is not offered for sale at from fifty cents to twenty dollars per acre; and improved land from five dollars to fifty dollars per acre. And even in Pulaski county, there are fine farms for sale at from five to one hundred dollars per acre, and that too, within easy distance of the city of Little Rock, where a great and growing market is offered for every product of the soil, and where land will rapidly increase in value, from the fact that Little Rock is destined to be, at an early day, the metropolis of the south-west, spreading out her suburbs for miles in every direction; and where farms are now, will soon be cut up and sold as town lots at so much per front foot.

"With the influx of immigration, lands will rise in value, markets will be nearer home, schools better, and better teachers; and, as a natural consequence crime diminished, and society better. And while all this is being accomplished, the value of lands in the entire State will improve so rapidly in value, that he who owns a few acres now may look forward, confidently, to the period when it shall be increased in value fifty fold." There never will be again, as good a time to secure Arkansas lands of various kinds, agricultural, fruit growing or mineral, as the present time. A great majority of those who own the land are poor, and desire, above every thing else to dispose of a portion of their lands; and the prices at which they will sell and favorable terms of payment, one third, one fourth, or less down, and the balance on long time, are sufficient inducements to attract immigration. New discoveries of minerals are being constantly made, and those discovered are generally under way of further development, and the mining interest generally, has received a new impetus. Though at this time, I know of coal property having a five foot vein of superior coal, well opened and ready for profitable operations, that is offered for $25 per acre; with buildings, improvements, and all located on the line of a projected rail road; while other coal lands can be bought for $10 to $20 per acre, which if located on the Ohio river, would sell for $1,000 per acre, for the reason that coal is in much better demand there now than in Arkansas. But who shall compute the demand in Arkansas, when the State becomes settled up, and the western States and territories are populated, as they will assuredly be. Nevertheless, where the timber is so scarce that the immigrant is obliged to go ten miles to get a stake to lariat his team while they feed, to say nothing of fuel or building timber.

The country west, north-west and south-west will, from the nature of things, have to depend, in a great measure, upon Arkansas for fuel, building and other timber. As further evidence of the value that will be placed upon timber lands in the future, statistical tables show that more than 150,000 acres of the best timber in America, are cut every year, to supply the demand for railway sleepers alone; and that the locomotives in the United States consume $56,000,000 worth of wood yearly. The best of brick clay is abundant all over the State; limestone rock, and all kinds of building stone, even to marble, are to be found in various localities. Building materials, such as shingles, laths, doors, sashes and blinds are to be obtained in all the towns, and the settler can easily and cheaply erect himself a house. Everything which can be produced in the United States, can here be produced in super-abundance, except the ice of Alaska, the rice of Carolina, and the oranges of Florida. In every county, vegetables, fruits and grains can be grown of fine quality, and in great abundance. We are about midway between the hot region of the south, and frozen plains of the north, giving us a climate not only delightful and salubrious, but enables the farmer to devote the entire year to plowing and preparing his soil for the various crops, and the great variety of crops here are an important consideration.

Every State must have one or more staple crops to depend upon for bringing money into the purse for taxes, etc. Illinois staple is corn and wheat; Minnesota, wheat; Wisconsin, wheat and pine lumber; Iowa, wheat and corn. Missouri has a greater number of staple crops, wheat, corn, hemp, tobacco, and mules. Arkansas' staple is cotton, in addition, stock, fruit, corn and tobacco, will constitute great staples.

"The following statement shows the status of British importations of cotton for the years named:

	1850.	1860.	1870.
	Pounds.	Pounds.	Pounds.
United States	493,153,112	1,115,890,608	716,245,040
Brazil	30,299,982	17,286,864	63,691,680
Mediteranean	18,931,414	44,036,608	153,228,320
British East Indies	118,872,742	204,141,168	341,599,776
British West Indies	228,913	1,050,784	
Other countries	2,090,698	8,532,720	61,606;832
Total	663,576,861	1,398,938,752	1.336,371,648

"The increase of ten years, through earnest and persistent efforts of European cotton supply associations, in India, Egypt, and Brazil, has been less than that made in the United States, in the single year 1870, over the previous crop. It is evident that no stimulation of production elsewhere will destroy our foreign market, and manifest to the most superficial observer that, as the manufacture increases in this country and the proportion for export diminishes, the more indispensible to foreign manufacturers will be that surplus. The quality of our cotton, the indubitable superiority to that of India, will make it a necessity to Europeans who would compete with the manufactures of the United States in the markets of the world. It is evidently the destiny of this country to take a large share in the business of supplying the world with manufactured cotton, a result to which the quality of the staple and the inventive genius and skill of Americans will largely contribute. The price per pound of the cotton exported from this country for the last eleven years, ending June 30, 1871, is presented in the following statement:

1861.	1862.	1863.	1864.	1865.	1866.	1867.	1868.	1869.	1870.	1871.
cents.	cents.	cents.	cents.	cents.	cents.	cents.	cents.	cents.	cents.	cents.
10 1-10	23 8-10	61 2-10	83 5-10	86 5-10	42 5-10	30 1-10	19 2-10	24 9-10	23 4-10	14 8-10

"The largest returns for a single year's exportation ever made were those for the year ending June 30, 1866; a portion of the cotton having been produced in 1865, and the remainder brought forth from the hidden stores of previous years, all realizing the sum of $274,960.453. The next largest amount realized was for the crop of 1869, sold in 1870, amounting to $224,121,191. The crop of 1870 brought $216,889,570."

The crop of 1871, now being sold, will perhaps average about nineteen cents per pound; and it is not likely that cotton will ever bring a less price than fifteen cents per pound. One man, besides growing grain, vegetables and fruits sufficient for himself and family, can cultivate ten acres in cotton, which, in this State, will make him ten bales, and at fifteen cents per pound, or \$69 $\frac{90}{100}$ per bale, (an average bale is 466 pounds) will amount to the sum of \$699. Now, where is there a State in the north or northwest that one man can do as well as that? His children, from five years up, can be efficiently employed in picking; and then he can take his two horse wagon and in three or four loads haul it to market and get the money, for it is always cash. But if the immigrant wants to raise corn, he can produce from forty to seventy-five bushels to the acre, and receive from fifty cents to $1 25 per bushel, or he can raise stock, or fruit, or vegetables, and his profits will be large; and besides there has never been, or ever likely to be, an over-supply of either of the above crops, that, as a result, would make their growing unremunerative.

Much has been said and written about ku-kluxism and the spirit of disloyalty in the south; and many sensational dispatches have passed over the wires to the prejudice of the southern people. Yet, I have taken a very close view of the inner life of the inhabitants of old *Arkansas*, and find much to approve. I have seen no violation of the law, heard of no outrage, no disturbance of the public peace that might not have taken place anywhere else. The people, everywhere, are found attending to their own private affairs, and anxious only to prosecute their several avocations. There does not exist in Arkansas any spirit of discontent, nor any desire to break up the present order of things. In fact, the people have no time to devote to parties or politics. Nor should it be forgotten that the people most eagerly desire immigration, and will welcome the new comer, be he yankee or foreigner. And further, no one need feel any hesitation in inducing others to come to this State for fear of failure. All can rest assured that the chances for commencing at the foot of the ladder, and growing in prosperity with the State as it must grow up to take its position among the foremost in point of wealth and population with the richest and most influential States of the Mississippi valley, are nowhere better. And to the man of means, we will just first say, that business enterprises are so profitable that money commands two per cent. a month in a great many instances, the legal rate, ten per cent. not being equal to the large profits derived from some business enterprises, and the security, the best in the world—real estate—constantly increasing in value.

HOW TO GET TO ARKANSAS.

In the first place, it may be well to remark that persons desiring to immigrate here ought to select their locality or county, and by looking at the map can see, most likely, the route to travel to reach that place.

But this State is easy of access by boat from any point on the Mississippi or Ohio rivers. Steamboats leave weekly St. Louis, Memphis and New Orleans, on the Mississippi river, for Little Rock, connecting at the latter place with a tri-weekly line of boats to Fort Smith and all points up the river; and at the mouth of White river, with a line of packets for all points on White and Black rivers to Batesville. A weekly line of boats also leave Pittsburg, Cincinnati and Louisville, on the Ohio river, for all points on the Arkansas, White, Black, Ouachita, Red and St. Francis rivers. Boats from the Mississippi, make regular trips to Bayou Bartholomew, Red, Ouachita, St. Francis and other navigable streams in the State. Immigrants from Europe will find it convenient to take passage to New Orleans, and thence by the Mississippi to any point they may wish to reach in the State, or by coming to Little Rock, can go by steamboat, rail or stage to any portion of the State. At present Little Rock can only be reached by rail from Memphis, but by July first, the Cairo and Fulton railroad will be completed, affording railroad facilities from St. Louis or Cairo direct to Little Rock; and during the year, several additional lines of railroad will be in operation. Parties within four or five hundred miles of the State, would do well to bring their stock, wagons and household goods, for the reason that persons breaking up to move can never realize enough for these articles to replace them in a new place. If the immigrant wishes a conveyance to any town or county away from the river or railroad, he will at all times find willing settlers to convey him to any place he may desire. I am satisfied the immigrant will find a location suitable to his anticipations.

PRICES OF LABOR, ETC.

Good black hands, for field labor, can be obtained for $150 and board per year; white field hands command from $20 to $25 and board per month; black female labor, for house work, is in great abundance, and receive from $6 to $8 per month; laborers by the day, from $1 50 to $2 50; carpenters get from $3 to $4 per day; stone and brick masons, plasterers, cabinet workmen, blacksmiths and wagon makers receive from $3 to $6 per day. House rents in the cities and towns are generally high, by reason of their rapid growth and increasing demand for houses, but in the country houses are plenty and rent very low. Hats, boots, shoes, clothing, dry goods and groceries are as cheap here as any State in the west. Wood manufactured articles, such as wagons, buggies, plows and furniture, are higher at present here than on the Ohio river; but, as all raw material and fuel necessary for their manufacture are here, of the best quality and in great abundance, these articles will be made here, and sold lower than the imported article. As an instance of prices now, White Water wagons are sold for $125; common bedsteads, that cost, in Cincinnati $3 to $4 by the hundred, retail here at $6 to $7 each; allowing 50 per cent. for freight and insurance, makes them cost $4 50 to $6 each. Here is an item for furniture manufacturers. The freight and insurance alone, to say nothing of the difference in the cost of the lumber, will make a handsome profit to Arkansas factories; and who will contend that such an outrage upon the laws of trade can long exist? Our advantages need only to be known by the outside world to be taken advantage of at once.

PROFITS ACCRUING FROM LABOR.

Many farmers in this State realized last year, a net income from their crops, of from five thousand to twenty thousand dollars and in some cases even more; and in many instances, tenants with only the assistance of their families, have realized for their portion of the crop from nine hundred to twelve hundred dollars. It must be remembered that about one-third of the cleared land in the State has laid idle since the war, for want of tenants or laborers; and these same idle lands will produce one bale of cotton, or fifty to seventy-five bushels of corn to the acre, and in many instances, the owners will furnish land, stock, tools, seed and feed, receiving at gathering time his part of the crop, absolutely furnishing every thing needful to make a crop (labor excepted) for a small compensation, besides giving six to eight months time to pay that small sum. One mans' labor in the north-west may produce 2000 bushels of corn, worth thirty-five cents a bushel, amounting to $700. The same labor here will produce a crop worth $1000 to $1,500, because the average price of corn in this State for the next five years will be about $1,00 per bushel, and cotton from $75 to $100 per bale. Then again, the winters of the north eat up the fruits of the summer's labor. Every grain, fruit, or vegetable that can be grown in the north, can be produced here, indeed their quality is improved here. No better business in the United States is offered to the enterprising farmer than to engage in the growing of fruits in Arkansas, here they come in bearing earlier, produce larger crops, with fewer total failures, and command larger prices than probably in any other section of the Union, with a certainty of remunerative prices in the future; rendered so, by the admirable situation of Arkansas. Apples at this date, February

20th, selling for $8 00 per barrel in Little Rock and other places.

"In the eastern and north-western States they all try to avoid a northern exposure. Our country is somewhat differently situated. This is the only part of the United States protected against violent winds. The mountains which shield it run east and west. The Ozark mountains running from the Indian Nation through Missouri to near St. Louis, performing the same office which the Alps do to Italy. This is indeed, as to climate, the Italy of the United States;" giving to Arkansas the most equable temperature of any State, therefore, rendering fruit culture a safe and lucrative business.

That the various kinds of grasses will grow finely in this State, is a demonstrated fact. Annual grasses need not be mentioned, but timothy, clover, red top, the standard grasses; they yield two tons to the acre, worth twenty dollars per ton; besides furnishing the best of pasture from October to April; the bottom lands must be pastured until May, to prevent falling down.

The lumber interest is naturally suggested to the mind by the immense forest growth. It is not unusual for a single pine to make two thousand feet of lumber. The black walnut timber of the State is of great value, and only awaits capital and labor to add greatly to the commercial wealth. St. Louis, Memphis and New Orleans afford good markets for lumber of all kinds.

STATE LANDS.

"The lands belonging to the State are swamp and overflowed lands, granted to the State by Congress in 1850; of these, there remain unsold about one million acres, divided into first and second class. The first class comprises those lying within six miles of a navigable stream, and are sold at seventy-five cents per acre. The second class are those lying more than that distance from navigable streams, and are sold at fifty cents per acre. This grant comprises some of the finest lands in the State."

INTERNAL IMPROVEMENT LANDS.

"Five hundred thousand acres were donated to the State by the general government in 1841, for the use of internal improvements in the State. They were selected with great care, and comprise the best lands then unsold. A portion of these lands are yet subject to entry. They are scattered over the entire State, and are sold by the State at $1 25 per acre, on a credit of one, two, three, four and five years, with interest payable annually at six per cent.

SEMINARY LANDS.

There was also donated by Congress, to this State, for the purpose of establishing a seminary of learning in this State, seventy-two sections of land, which were carefully selected from the most valuable tracts. These lands are sold by the State at $2 per acre, upon the same terms as the internal improvement lands, except that the interest is ten per cent per annum.

SALINE LANDS.

Congress donated to the State a certain amount of land contiguous to the various salt springs. A part has been sold and the remainder is subject to entry at $1 25 per acre, one fifth cash and the balance on time.

Next to Little Rock, the most thriving cities in the State are Fort Smith, situated in the lap of the coal field of the State, surrounded by forests of valuable timber is shortly to become a large manufacturing city. Pine Bluff, situated in the cotton planting region of the Arkansas river, is a flourishing city. Helena, on the Mississippi, is to become a very important place. Camden, on the Ouachita river, will be a large city, on the line of two or three important rail roads. Batesville, Van Buren, Fayetteville, Jacksonport, Dardanelle, Eunice, Washington and Hot Springs, will all become large places; they are now good business points. In addition, there are many other thriving towns, desirable localities for business enterprises.

MINING COMPANIES.

SPADRA COAL AND IRON COMPANY'S MINES.

This property consists of fifteen hundred and eighty-five acres of land, lying on the Arkansas river, in Johnson county, one hundred miles by land from Little Rock. Spadra creek bisects the land and affords water, the greater portion of the year, sufficient for boats and barges to enter up to the coal pits, receive their cargo and depart. The whole of this tract is underlaid by a bed of very superior coal, thirty-two feet under ground, and, at the main shaft, is from three to six feet thick of clear coal, with an excellent roof and solid floors. The coal will be conveyed to market on barges propelled by tow-boats.

These mines are not only 1,100 miles nearer New Orleans than the Pittsburg mines are, but on a better river, one that never freezes and is seldom obstructed by low water, with no falls, canals or locks to demand toll. The company also design erecting iron works for the reduction of the iron ore on the property, limestone for flux being in great abundance only twelve miles below. The value of these coal and iron lands can be better appreciated by the fact that the attention of foreign capitalists have been attracted to this property, and already advances, at a low rate of interest, have been offered from parties in Europe, for the purpose of making further developments and pushing forward the enterprise, showing by their offer that they have confidence in the great richness of our minerals. And further, an estimate of the amount of coal this bed contains to the acre, shows 5,400 tons, which, multiplied by 1,585 acres, makes the grand total of 8,127,000 tons of coal underlying this tract, and it is safe to calculate that the coal can be mined and sold at a net profit of two dollars per ton, which will make the clear profits of these coal lands the enormous sum of $16,254,000. And it is safe to say that this property, once under successful operation, will pay six per cent. interest on a capital of $2,000,000.

The coal proves to be rich in all the elements that particularly fit it for heating and manufacturing purposes, and of just the quality needed to work iron, being free from sulphur. The iron ore, also, proves to be carbonate iron ore, the same quality as at Staffordshire, England, the best in the world for making steel, etc., and existing in immense beds in close proximity to the coal, renders it still more valuable. The company have already spent fifty thousand dollars in developing the coal interest, building barges, buying tow-boats, machinery, tools, etc. The favorable situation of the mines will enable the company to successfully compete for the trade of the lower Mississippi river country.

The coal fields of Arkansas are as extensive as those of Pennsylvania, and the quality equally as good. And once our coal mines are opened, Arkansas will be able to supply coal much cheaper to people residing on the lower Mississippi than they have been paying; and we predict that in a short time Arkansas coal will be as familiar in southern cities as Pittsburg coal is at this time. A practical operation, like the Spadra company, will be an invitation to capitalists of other States and of Europe to invest in and build up mining and manufacturing establishments of every kind throughout the entire domain of Arkansas; and further, prove to the world not only the great richness of our State in minerals, but the great advantage for mining and delivering the products of the mines and manufactories to the markets of the world. And the tillers of the soil will have in these enterprises a nucleus for a home market for every product of the soil, thereby benefitting all alike, and by that means adding greatly to the wealth of the State. The three great wants of the State are capital, that shall be active; labor, that shall be judiciously employed, and population that shall possess the land and make it vocal with the hum of busy industry.

AMERICAN ZINC COMPANY, OF NEW YORK.

This company, with a working capital of $1,000,000, are in successful operation upon a two thousand acre tract of mineral land of great value, which they own in Sharp county, formerly a part of Lawrence county. This company, for labor alone, pay out every month over $2,000. They have erected good mills, fine houses and are supplied with splendid machinery, and already have several tons of zinc and copper ore ready for shipment. They also have lead mines in operation, a smelter, and, in fact, every thing necessary, and in good order, requisite for succesful operations, and are now making as fine lead as can be made anywhere. Their ores of sulphuret of zinc contain 63 per cent. of metal. The company's works are a nucleus for a home market for the products of the surrounding country, and at the same time affording cheap living to the hands employed at the works and mines, buying beef at five cents per pound, eggs ten cents per dozen, chickens twelve and a half cents apiece, and other articles at an equally cheap rate. Every mining company or factory in operation in the State adds greatly to the number of non-producers, thereby stimulating the farming community to a greater extent by reason of the home market afforded. What must be the result when the great and diversified mineral resources of the State become generally known, properly estimated, developed and worked.

THE OUITA COAL COMPANY

Own a valuable tract of coal land, situated in Pope county, directly on the Little Rock and Fort Smith railroad, and distant from Little Rock eighty miles. This company is now successfully working a bed of coal, three feet in thickness, of a superior quality; and from the close proximity of these mines to the railroad, which will be completed to a point west of these mines by the first of March, will enable the Ouita Coal Company to supply Little Rock and other places with coal at a comparatively low price.

ARKANSAS NEWSPAPERS.

List of newspapers, politics of each, and where published in Arkansas. Those marked D. are Democratic; R., Republican; N., neutral.

Name.	Town.	County.
Times, D, weekly	Hamburg	Ashley.
Democrat, D, weekly	DeWitt	Arkansas.
Record, D, weekly	Bellefonte	Boone.
Advocate, R, weekly	Harrison	"
Gazette, R, weekly	Wittsburg	Cross.
Flower, R, weekly	Magnolia	Columbia.
Wide-Awake, D, weekly	Lewisburg	Conway.
Press, D, weekly	Van Buren	Crawford.
Standard, D, weekly	Arkadelphia	Clark.
Southwestern Republican, R, w'kly,	Arkadelphia	"
Monticellonian, D, weekly	Monticello	Drew.
Courier, R, weekly	Hot Springs	Hot Springs.
Telegraph, D, weekly	Washington	Hempstead.
Times, D, weekly	Batesville	Independence.
Republican, R, weekly	Batesville	"
Press, D, weekly	Pine Bluff	Jefferson.
Republican, R, weekly	Pine Bluff	"
Statesman, R, weekly	Jacksonport	Jackson.
Democrat, D, weekly	Camden	Ouachita.
Journal, R, weekly	Camden	"
Citizen, D, weekly	Des Arc	Prairie.
Tribune, R, weekly	Russellville	Pope.
Journal, R, weekly	DeValls Bluff	Prairie.
Gazette, D, daily and weekly	Little Rock	Pulaski.
Republican, R. daily and weekly	Little Rock	"

9

Name.	Town.	County.
Journal, R, daily and weekly	Little Rock	Pulaski.
Educational Journal, N, monthly	Little Rock	"
World, D, daily and weekly	Helena	Phillips.
Clarion, R, daily and weekly	Helena	"
Shield, R, weekly	Helena	"
Express, R, weekly	Pocahontas	Randolph.
Courier, R, weekly	Pocahontas	"
Times, D, weekly	Forest City	St. Francis.
Herald, D, tri-weekly and weekly	Fort Smith	Sebastian.
New Era, R, tri-weekly and w'kly	Fort Smith	"
Patriot, R, weekly	Fort Smith	"
Western Independent, N, weekly	Fort Smith	"
Bulletin, D, weekly	Augusta	Woodruff.
Sentinel, R, weekly	Augusta	"
Record, D, weekly	Searcy	White.
Tribune, R, weekly	Searcy	"
Democrat, D, weekly	Fayetteville	Washington.
Echo, R, weekly	Fayetteville	"
News, R, weekly	Fayetteville	"
Times, D, weekly	Oceola	Mississippi.
Chronicle, D, weekly	Dardanelle	Yell.

In addition to these, there are two or three monthly real estate journals, published as advertising mediums. In the list given above, there are twenty-one Democrat, twenty-three Republican, and two neutral, making forty-six in all. Three more Republican papers are just starting. The publishers of either of the journals will cheerfully respond to inquiries of knowledge about the State.

HOMESTEAD EXEMPTION.

The homestead law of the State is more liberal than that of any State in the Union. By a provision of the Constitution, adopted by the Constitutional Convention, 11th of February, 1868, and subsequently ratified by the people, one hundred and sixty acres of land are exempted from execution. The benefits of this exemption, should the head of the family be removed by death, inure to his widow while she remains unmarried, also to his children during their minority. The Constitution further provides: "The personal property of any resident citizen of the State to the value of two thousand dollars, to be selected by such resident, shall be exempted from sale or execution, or other final process of any court issued for the collection of any debt contracted after the adoption of this Constitution. Every homestead, not exceeding one hundred and sixty acres of land and the dwelling and appurtenances thereon, to be selected by the owner thereof, and not in a town, city or village; or, in lieu thereof, at the option of the owner, any lot in a city, town or village, with the dwelling theron, owned and occupied by any resident of this State, and not exceeding the value of $5,000, shall be exempted from sale or execution, or any other final process of any court."

Further, it says: "The homestead of a family, after the death of the owner thereof, shall be exempt from the payment of his debts, in all cases during the minority of his children, and also, so long as his widow shall remain unmarried, unless she shall be the owner of a homestead in her own right." It also provides, that the property of a female, before marriage, shall be held by her in her own right, as long as she shall so elect, to be disposed of by her as she shall deem proper. These provisions of the Constitution, it will be seen, provide against the possibility of any one being distressed or deprived of a home.

LIMITATION OF CIVIL SUITS.

"All open accounts are barred in three years; all liquidated demands, notes, etc., are barred in five years, except mortgages and judgments.

IN CONCLUSION.

I think Arkansas has a great future. We anchored in Arkansas over a year ago—have tried it in sickness, in health, and in adversity, and have decided, beyond a doubt, that we like Arkansas. "Nor has this conclusion been leaped at; it is not the mind enthused by picturesque scenery, balmy breezes, and glorious sunshine. It is not the conclusion of one determined to be pleased, but it is the result of reason—a deduction fairly

drawn by our experience, and confirmed by the experience of others." We are proud of her "illimitable resources." We like her diversified soil, prolific in all the elements of re-production, and which, if ever so gently "tickled" witn a hoe, "will smile with a harvest." We like her "balmy breezes, laden with the invigorating nutriment of pure air, bearing healing on its wing." We like the glorious beauty of her moon light, the soft tranquility of her sunset, and the magnificence of her dawn. But there are more practical reasons why we like this State. Arkansas is a good poor man's country. Here, he can live with less wear of muscle and brain than in most of the States. Here, by reasonable thrift and economy, he can acquire a competency, for which he would have toiled in vain upon the cold plains of the north, or the over-crowded lands of the east. Here, the investment of a small capital pays a better interest than elsewhere. Here, the frugal farmer can at all times have something to sell, for which he will get the highest price, by reason of his being situated half-way between the warm sugar lands of the gulf, and the bleak prairies of the north. Here, while men can almost live without labor, industry meets with a commensurate reward, and nature responds promptly to every demand made upon her resources, and more than all else, is the vast margin left to the development of the soil.

"In short, amid all her vast blessings we have not yet found one evil which may not be rectified by time and progress, or so much ameliorated by the genius of man as to be unworthy of a reckoning." We will not further attempt to describe the natural advantages of this State, but we do say, that no man can suggest a substantial good this country does not possess. For soil, climate, water, drainage, stone, timber, coal, grasses, grazing, fruit-growing and general farming purposes," Arkansas is unrivalled, and we think unequalled. "These items, the sure basis of wealth, have attracted many thousands to Arkansas since the war, and immigration, though last year large, is this year larger than ever," and still they come; and be it known, that Arkansas is not full; still within her domain lie millions of acres of land untilled. And that is not all. This country is not only rich in all the elements of agricultural life, but possesses vast stores of valuable minerals, easy of access, in a country beautiful to look upon. Think of such a country! What a land will this be, when our rail roads are completed—when daily trains come thundering along, through all this splendid country? Why, fifty dollars per acre will be the value of these lands then, now selling for five. Fifty, yes one hundred and fifty dollars, much of these lands will command per acre.

We say to our restless and dissatisfied neighbors of other States, and to the enterprising, but heavily burdened emigrants of Europe, do as we have done, come to Arkansas, and you will soon like it as we do. Take it for all in all the State of Arkansas, is perhaps the most inviting portion of the American continent. The sun never shone on more fertile soil, or more smiling landscapes of water, timber, and varied scenery. Since coming to Arkansas, now nearly two years, I have seen a greater portion of the country and people, and having seen a great deal of the country west of the Mississippi river, I know of no State where as rich lands, fruitful in all the products of the soil, underlaid with beds of valuable minerals, with advantages of a healthy climate, good water, plenty of timber, as can be found in Arkansas, are offered to settlers on such favorable terms, and where happy, peaceable and prosperous homes can be established for themselves and their children. Yes, Arkansas has great advantages, and it only needs the facts correctly laid before the people to call men and capital thither.

I have endeavored neither to under estimate nor over rate the resources and advantages of the State. I may have committed errors, but they were in judgment, not of intention. This State is, without doubt, the most inviting to the farmer, capitalist, mechanic and laborer of any State in the Union. As the advantages and resources are superior, we think, to any other section; and we would recommend it to all seeking new homes to benefit their condition in life. Arkansas is attracting more attention than probably any other State at this

time. But the end is not yet, this State has only begun to reap the benefits of her commanding situation; and with more general information known abroad in regard to her resources, she will reap a corrosponding increase of wealth and prosperity.

The location of Little Rock upon a beautiful upland, rising in gentle slopes stretching away in enchanting landscapes, having everywhere the most inviting sites for beautiful homes, with majestic views of the Arkansas river and valley; and above and beyond all, made glorious by an atmosphere pure and health-inspiring, visited by cooling winds in summer, and gentle rays of sun shine in winter; dotted here and there with fine residences, with wide yards surrounded by extensive gardens, interspersed with Magnolia trees, rose bushes and fragrant flowers; with streets regularly laid out, and scrupulously kept clean, wide side-walks, shaded by the beautiful mulberry, maple and catalpa trees. Think of such beautiful sites, ye rent-burdened citizens of crowded cities, and you over crowded artisans and mercenaries of manufacturing districts.

There Little Rock sits, proudly in the Arkansas valley, in the center of the State, surrounded by a country rich in soil, rich in mineral wealth, rich in timber resources; on the great highways from the Atlantic to the Pacific, from the north to the South ; the rail road center of the State, the capital of a great State, the commercial and manufacturing center for the south-west and one of the "future great cities of the south-west."

Let her citizens be true to her interest, improve the advantages she now possesses, encourage and build up her manufactures, extend her trade and commerce, foster and encourage immigration, open new lines of travel, and she will outstrip all her rivals. To the immigrant we extend a cordial welcome. To the capitalist we promise remunerative business.

www.ingramcontent.com/pod-product-compliance
Lightning Source LLC
LaVergne TN
LVHW021417110826
845150LV00007B/1969

* 9 7 8 1 4 2 5 5 0 9 5 0 7 *